Young People and Work

Research studies commissioned and managed by
Maureen Colledge, Geoffrey Llewellyn and Vernon Ward,
Office of Manpower Services Commission

London: Her Majesty's Stationery Office

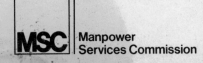
MSC Manpower Services Commission

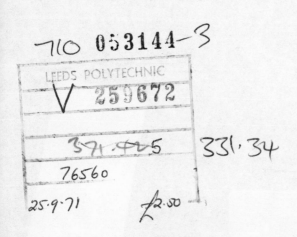
ISBN 0 11 887502 7

Contents

1 Chapter   Introduction   *Page*   5

2   Summary of the main findings   7

PART I   **Unemployed young people**   11

3   Experience of unemployment   12

4   Youth unemployment – a brief investigation of the causes   21

5   Attitudes towards publicly-funded programmes and other forms
                of help for the young unemployed   25

PART II   **From school to work**   31

6   Education and the preparation of young people for work   32

7   Recruitment   38

8   Young people at work   44

9   Training and further education   54

PART III   **Appendix and details**   59

                Technical Appendix   60

                References   76

                Bibliography   78

1.1 The Manpower Services Commission's Working Party on Young People and Work was established in response to the pressing need to provide alternatives to unemployment for the historically very high numbers of young people throughout the country who are, or are likely to be, unemployed. Such 'alternatives' were to be of a sort which would improve the ability of young people to find, and keep, jobs in the normal labour market and the programme of measures, which the Government has decided to implement, was designed with this requirement in mind.

1.2 Although unemployment among young people must be looked at in the context of unemployment for workers of all ages, the commission considers that it is a problem which merits special attention. This is, primarily, because:

(a) the national work force can be renewed only through the recruitment of young people; and

(b) unemployment during this crucial stage of a person's life may do long-term damage to both the individual and society.

1.3 From the outset it was clear to the Working Party that it needed to address itself to a number of basic issues. These included:

(a) whether youth unemployment was akin to unemployment generally, and would fall when that fell, or was influenced by factors which might cause it to be prolonged as general unemployment fell;

(b) whether certain groups of young people suffer unemployment disproportionately and, if so, to what extent their disadvantages required particular solutions; and

(c) the extent to which the then current measures designed to help unemployed young people find work were meeting the needs of both young people and employers.

1.4 Previous research had examined the position of young people in the labour market from two related angles. It was concerned first with the general level of provision of vocational guidance information in schools, with the amount of induction and longer-term training undertaken by employers, and with the general efficiency of the process whereby young people entered work; and secondly, with the manner in which the general level of provision was differentially available to, or consumed by, different groups of young people.

1.5 Several studies referred to in this booklet, some carried out under the auspices of government agencies, have focused on these two aspects of the issue and, in general, concluded that the overall level of provision has been inadequate. They have noted also that the young person's experience of the labour market is affected by his or her social environment.

1.6 In view of the way in which the situation facing young people had worsened in recent years, the Working Party commissioned four pieces of survey and analysis to supplement and update the existing information on these issues. The main concerns of the surveys were:

(a) What are the characteristics of currently unemployed young people and how are they looking for jobs?

(b) What factors are causing youth unemployment and what are the future prospects for young people trying to get jobs?

(c) What are the attitudes of young people and employers to schemes to help young unemployed people?

(d) What is the present position of young people in the general labour market, with which groups do they compete for jobs, and for what jobs do employers recruit them?

(e) How do young people find jobs, what advice are they given about jobs they might enter, and how do employers recruit them ?

(f) What are the attitudes of young people toward the world of work and what are employers' attitudes towards young people ?

(g) What experience do young people have of training and further educaton and what are their attitudes to them ?

1.7 The following work was commissioned by the Working Party:

The 'Employers Survey', undertaken by Industrial Facts and Forecasting Ltd, interviewed over 1,100 senior representatives of employing organisations drawn from all sectors of industry, except central Government. The fieldwork was carried out in November 1976 and the enquiry focused on employers' recruitment practices and their attitudes towards young people.

The 'Young People Survey', undertaken by NOP Market Research Ltd, interviewed a national random sample of over 3,000 16 to 19 year olds. Fieldwork was carried out in November 1976 and the survey asked young people about their experience of education, work and unemployment and their attitudes towards various actual and possible government sponsored schemes aimed at helping them.

The 'Unemployed Survey', undertaken by Social and Community Planning Research, interviewed 550 unemployed 16 to 18 year olds who had been previously contacted by the MSC through ten selected Unemployment Benefit Offices at which they were registered. The fieldwork was carried out in January 1977 and the topics covered were similar to those in the Young People Survey, although it was possible to examine them in rather greater detail.

The 'Training Survey' was a special analysis of the National Training Survey carried out in 1975 by Research Services Ltd. on behalf of the Training Services Agency. Information was available regarding current and first employment, and experiences of and attitudes to training. The subset analysed for the purpose of the Working Party amounted to some 7,000 16 to 24 year olds.

Further details of all four surveys are included in the Technical Appendix.

1.8 This document draws together the results of the four studies in order to provide a coherent picture of the current employment situation facing young people. *Part I* gives the findings on unemployed young people and how they could be helped. *Part II* gives the findings on the general position of young people entering the work force. *Part III* gives details of how the surveys were undertaken, the questions asked, the characteristics of the samples, and the coding of occupation and industry details.

1.9 The results reported in this publication do not cover all the data which was provided by these surveys. The complete 'data set' is however still under analysis and interested parties are invited to contact the MSC* if they wish to pursue any points mentioned in the publication, or if they wish to explore the possibility of obtaining additional information.

*Manpower Services Commission, Selkirk House, 166 High Holborn, London WC1V 6PF.

Chapter 2

Summary of the main findings

Part I – Unemployed young people

a) 12% of 16–19 year olds in the survey were unemployed. Rates of unemployment were highest among 16 and 17 year olds, reflecting the increasing difficulties of school leavers in finding work. (3.3 – 3.4)

b) The family backgrounds of the unemployed showed that a disproportionate number came from families in the C2/DE social classes* and had fathers employed in manual occupations. A high incidence was found in the Unemployed Survey of unemployment among friends and other members of the family: 79% had friends unemployed, 14% had fathers unemployed, 21% had a brother or sister unemployed and 19% lived in households where no-one was in full-time employment. (3.6 – 3.9)

c) Many of the unemployed had had little success at school and, despite saying that they had enjoyed their last two years, most had left school at the earliest opportunity; less than one-third had been advised to stay on. Over half left school with no qualifications and the majority of the remainder left with only CSEs of lower than grade 1. (3.11 – 3.13)

d) A few had special difficulties – disablement, illiteracy, educational subnormality. Their prospects of finding a job are poor at best; with high levels of unemployment they are considerably worsened. (3.14 – 3.16)

e) The periods of time young people are spending on the unemployed register are increasing. The unqualified are likely to stay unemployed longest and they are likely to suffer unemployment more frequently. (3.17 – 3.21)

f) The unemployed are looking hard for jobs. Among other things, they are looking in newspapers, visiting the Careers Office, Jobcentre or Employment Office and approaching employers directly. (3.22 – 3.25)

g) The majority of the unemployed young people had applied for six or more jobs; very few had been offered and had refused a job. While 42% had expected to find a job easily at the start, only 16% now did. (3.30 – 3.31)

h) Evidence suggests youth unemployment is part of the general employment problem but that an upturn in the economy, which would help reduce the general level of unemployment, might still leave many young people unemployed because employers are more attracted to other workers, especially those with experience. A further fall in business activity might cause increased unemployment among young people as redundancies occur based on either ability or the principle of 'last in, first out'. (4.3 – 4.22)

i) Employers did not have a high regard for the existing Government measures to aid young people, claiming that they were too numerous, badly publicised and changed too frequently. They thought the most useful scheme was the Work Experience Programme with its emphasis on increasing young people's knowledge of work. (5.3 – 5.6)

j) Unemployed young people generally thought there was not enough done to help them. About half were willing to go back to school or on to college; 40% said there was some training they wanted to do; and over half, especially the girls, were willing to undertake community or voluntary work; 40% said they would be prepared to move if a job were offered to them in another part of the country. From their answers to questions about the type of help they would appreciate it seems, however, that a less 'official' approach may be needed to help some unemployed young people. (5.10 – 5.24)

*See Technical Appendix Section III for a description of the social class groups.

k) Young people rated as the most important features of a Government training or work experience scheme opportunities:

(i) to learn a skill for a job which had already been chosen;

(ii) for on-the-job training;

(iii) for help from a sympathetic supervisor; and

(iv) for instruction in how to make a good impression of an employer. (5.25 – 5.30)

**Part II —
From school to work**

a) Many young people in their last few years at school said they were apprehensive about their prospects of getting a job when they leave. (6.12)

b) For those who had left, experience of work whilst at school smoothed the process of finding and settling in a job. However, most young people only gained such experience through their own efforts; few mentioned experiencing work through programmes arranged by their schools. (6.13 – 6.16)

c) Of those who were unemployed, nearly half had played truant in their last two years at school and 29% had stayed away several times; 11% had had two or more periods of illness of a month or more off school. Evidence suggested absence due to illness may have affected their ability to get work but the effect of truancy is less clear. (6.17–6.20)

d) The last few years at school are a time when young people form their ideas about work, and when receipt of advice and information can be an important influence. The majority of young people had received help and advice from a careers teacher, careers officer and their parents, and most had found the help useful. For the unemployed, parental advice was more important that that from the careers teacher or careers officer. (6.24 – 6.31)

e) Two-thirds of employers thought young job applicants were not well briefed about the job, the firm or how to behave at the interview. They place the main responsibility for the latter on schools and careers officers, and responsibility for briefing young people about the firm and the job on careers officers and themselves. (6.32 – 6.34)

f) At head office level, employers were generally critical of the relationship between school and work, feeling that many people in education regard industry as 'second best'. They wanted higher priority to be given to careers education, and more information about work given to school children. They said they are willing to develop stronger links with schools but realised there were many prejudices, on both sides, that needed to be overcome. (6.35 – 6.36)

g) Young people compete alongside applicants of all ages for most jobs – only apprenticeships are considered to be 'young people' jobs. (7.2)

h) Willingness and attitude to work are the main criteria by which employers judge recruits, although those applying to skilled and non-manual* jobs are expected to have a good basic standard of education. Although nearly half the employers thought there was no difference between young people and other recruits on these aspects, those that did see a difference were more likely to think young people compared unfavourably. (7.3 – 7.5)

*See Technical Appendix Section IV for a description of types of jobs included under occupational headings.

i) Employers said they turn down young applicants because of their attitude and personality, their appearance and manners, and their lack of basic education. Given a choice of recruits, many employers prefer others to young people, especially if they can upgrade existing employees or recruit experienced workers or housewives. (7.6 – 7.8)

j) While over 40% of employers thought the calibre of young applicants had not changed over the last five years, nearly one-third thought it had declined, especially among those applying for skilled manual jobs; 46% of employers could see no improvement at all in young applicants, while only 28% said they had seen no decline. They thought young people had improved in maturity and independence but had deteriorated in their attitude to work, in basic educational ability and in their dress and manners. (7.9 – 7.12)

k) Employers make little use of the Careers Office when seeking applicants of any age for jobs, though they do use it when specifically recruiting young people, especially to skilled and non-manual jobs. Newspaper advertisements are a major source for non-manual jobs, while for manual jobs young people are as often recruited through personal contacts and other informal methods as through the Careers Office. It seems many jobs which would be suitable for young people are not registered by employers with the Careers Service. (7.13 – 7.17)

l) About a third of employed young people in the surveys worked in manufacturing industries, with distribution, transport, communications and the other services sector accounting for substantial numbers. Around two-fifths of the boys entered apprenticeships and a similar number of girls entered clerical jobs. A comparison with past data shows that this pattern of employment has changed little over time. (8.2, 8.7)

m) The type of job a young person gets is linked to his or her qualifications, although about a third of young people in craft jobs had no qualifications. Evidence suggests a qualification 'screen' is used for many skilled and non-manual jobs, particularly by larger firms and the more office-based industries. (8.3 – 8.6)

n) Young people are known to change jobs more frequently than older workers. This could be due, in part, to 'job shopping' – trying out jobs to improve satisfaction, prospects, etc. Little evidence emerged of job dissatisfaction among young people, however, even among those whose jobs might be thought to be less interesting. The most frequent job changers were those now unemployed, and for these young people many of their moves had been made involuntarily, had resulted in a 'downgrading' in type of job, and, when made voluntarily, had been motivated often by a desire to improve pay and conditions, possibly as compensation for the less interesting nature of their jobs. (8.12 – 8.23)

o) Two-thirds of employers said they gave induction to new recruits, though only just over a third, mainly the larger firms, said they gave an induction specifically geared to young people. (9.2 – 9.4)

p) The surveys suggest that over 200,000 young people entering work each year receive no formal training. A third of the 16–24 year olds had received no formal training and two-thirds had received no further education. Girls and those with no qualifications were least likely to receive training. (9.5 – 9.9)

q) Skilled manual jobs stand out as providing systematic training, usually in the form of an apprenticeship combined with further education. Young people employed in small establishments were much less likely to undertake apprenticeships and more likely to receive no training at all. (9.10 – 9.14)

r) Most young people receive some help and assistance in learning their jobs – mainly through watching others, being taught or helped, being sent round departments, reading or making things for practice. (9.15)

s) Very few young people had tried to get training and failed, and few had been offered and rejected training. The majority said they would be willing to undertake training if it was offered to them, and a quarter would want to train for a different job. The benefits of training were seen as increased earnings, help in getting a better job and greater interest in, and satisfaction from, the job. (9.16 – 9.19)

PART I

Unemployed
young people

Chapter 3

Experience of Unemployment

Introduction

3.1 Department of Employment statistics show an increasing problem of unemployment among young people, both in absolute terms and relative to all other age groups. Registered unemployment among 16 to 17 year olds has risen by 120% between January 1972 and January 1977, compared with 45% for the working population as a whole. Furthermore, the proportion of unemployed 16 and 17 year olds has risen as a proportion of the total unemployed from 5.4% in January 1971 to 9% in January 1977, even excluding the young unemployed registered with the Employment Service Agency. Within the young unemployed total the proportion of girls has increased from 35% in January 1970, to 49% in January 1977; and the average length of time young people spend unemployed has increased, although average duration is still less than for older age groups.

3.2 The official statistics show, however, only the numbers of young unemployed people and do not tell us anything about their characteristics such as their family, social and educational backgrounds; about particular disadvantages which they may suffer; the frequency with which they have been unemployed; the actions they have taken to look for jobs; the types of jobs they look for; and how they pass their time whilst unemployed. This section presents findings from the surveys on these aspects.

Who are the young unemployed?

3.3 In the Young People Survey 12% (250) of the 16–19 year olds not in full-time education or training were unemployed and seeking work. They were split more or less equally between the sexes; the rates of unemployment were highest amongst 16 and 17 year olds (16% and 14% respectively) and in the North West (19%) and the North (16%).

3.4 The increasing difficulties faced by school-leavers in getting jobs are evident from the proportion of those in the surveys who had never been employed; 32% of the unemployed 16–19 year olds in the Training Survey had not had jobs. (The bulk of the interviewing for this survey was done in 1975 from July to September, the post school-leaving peak period for youth unemployment). In November 1976, 41% of the 16–19 year olds interviewed for the Young People Survey had never had a job and, whilst not necessarily typical of the unemployed generally, 39% of the 16–18 year olds in the January 1977 Unemployed Survey had not been employed. The bulk of these young people had left school the previous summer and had been looking for a job ever since.

3.5 Although based, in some cases, on rather small samples these findings are broadly similar to those indicated by the national unemployment statistics.

Family and social background

3.6 Many of the unemployed come from relatively 'disadvantaged' backgrounds. They are much more likely to come from families in the C2/DE social classes and have fathers employed in manual occupations than are the employed young people or those still in full-time education (see Technical Appendix for a comparison of the samples).

3.7 The Unemployed Survey paints an even gloomier picture. This sample was not strictly random and is probably more representative of the longer-term young unemployed and of those in deprived inner city areas. However, the family and social backgrounds of these young people illustrate the additional problems faced by some of the young unemployed. Most (93%) were living at home in what are quite large family units (the mean household size was 5.3 persons). There was a considerable amount of unemployment amongst other family members: 14% had fathers who were unemployed (this increased to 21% in Glasgow), 22% at least one unemployed brother or sister and 19% lived in households where no-one was in full-time work.

3.8 A survey of unemployed, disadvantaged young people (Reference 1), in 1969, found similar evidence of family problems. A high proportion of the young people interviewed were from large families, frequently with only one parent present; where both parents were present it was not unusual for the father to be unemployed. The young people frequently had at least one brother or sister on probation.

3.9 One in four (26%) of the young people in the Unemployed Survey said most or all of their friends were unemployed and nearly four in five (79%) had some friends unemployed; this reflects the concentration of unemployment in areas and among social groups.

3.10 Asked how their parents and friends felt about their being unemployed, most indicated that parents and friends were generally sympathetic and supportive. Typical replies were:

"They know it's the same for everyone."

"They feel sorry for me but it's no good being miserable about it."

"They don't think it's my fault."

"Mother is wonderful, she knows I'm trying to get a job."

Some parents were rather more concerned, however, and, at times, critical of their son's or daughter's unemployment. For example:

"Parents don't moan but they do say hurry up and get a job."

"They don't think much of it."

"Bad about it – me being about the house."

"Worried – think I should have got a job by now."

"Dad just goes mad and says why don't I get a job."

"It causes arguments at home."

"They feel very sorry for me and upset, and they don't want me to get into any trouble."

A minority had friends who were rather more flippant:

"They don't mind because they are unemployed, some of them don't want to work. They say they are all right on the labour exchange."

School experience

3.11 Most of the young people in the Unemployed Survey (75%) said they had enjoyed their last two years at school, though there were certain subjects they disliked, most commonly mathematics. Almost half had at some time played truant during their last two years at school and 82% had left at the earliest opportunity, giving as reasons that they had become tired of, or disliked, school and that they wanted to get a job. Those who left later gave as the most important reasons for leaving that they wanted to get a job and that they could not stay longer at the school, perhaps because they had reached the end of the course for which they had been studying. In some cases family pressure, usually for financial reasons, had been put on the young person to leave school.

3.12 Only 31% of the young people in the Unemployed Survey had been advised by someone to stay longer at school, and this advice appears to have been given more frequently to later leavers than to the early leavers. Parents and the class teacher most frequently advised the young people to stay on, usually so that they could sit exams or improve their education.

3.13 The unemployed young people were generally less successful at school. They were much more likely to have few or no qualifications than were either the young people in employment or those in full-time education (see Technical Appendix for a comparison of the samples). Just over half (53%) of those in the Unemployed Survey had no qualifications; 28% had only CSEs less than grade 1 and only 19% had one or more GCE 'O' level or CSE grade 1. The boys were more likely to have no qualification than the girls: 60% of the boys in the Unemployed Survey had no qualification compared with 46% of the girls.

Special difficulties

3.14 A small number seemed to have special difficulties. A National Survey of the Unemployed (2) carried out in November 1973 when unemployment was relatively low, found a higher proportion of the unemployed of all ages had some disability (registered or unregistered) than in the working population as a whole; 10% of the under 25s in the survey had some disability and a further 6% were 'not too strong' or 'in poor health'. In the Unemployed Survey 5% had attended a school for handicapped or ESN pupils in their last two years at school. (This was proportionally greater than national statistics for 15 and 16 year olds in the local education authority areas covered in the sample, though comparison is difficult because of differences in area size between the Survey's sample and LEAs.)

3.15 Other indications of disability emerged when young people were asked what they were doing to find work. The following comments were made on the use of the Jobcentre:

"Kind and helpful; they put me on the disabled list and gave me information about courses for disabled people."

"They said fill in a form. I can't read or write so they don't help me, they just leave me."

"He wasn't rude like some of them are, he tried to help me. Yes, that was the disablement one."

3.16 These comments represent a minority of the unemployed as a whole (quotes here came from a selection of 150 questionnaires), but they clearly show special needs. At a time of high unemployment such young people are likely to have even greater difficulties in getting a job than in more normal times.

Length of time spent unemployed and frequency of unemployment

3.17 In all three of the young people surveys, the average duration of unemployment was longer than that shown for the nearest Department of Employment count. (See Table 3.1 for comparisons). There are a number of possible reasons for this. Both the random sample surveys included some unregistered unemployed and evidence from our Young People Survey suggests that a small number of young people do not register until their second or third week of unemployment. The DE counts only record complete and uninterrupted periods (for example if a person leaves the register because of illness and then rejoins when he or she has recovered, only the period since re-registering will be counted). The much longer average durations of unemployment for those in the Unemployed Survey probably reflect the larger proportion in the sample coming from depressed inner city areas.

3.18 The young people surveys showed a strong relationship between lack of qualifications and length of time spent unemployed. Those with few or no qualifications were likely to remain unemployed for longer than those who were better qualified. In the Unemployed Survey, for example, 61% of those with no qualifications had been unemployed for more than 6 months, compared with 49% of those with only CSEs less than grade 1 and 43% of those with GCE 'O' level or equivalent.

3.19 Excluding those still looking for their first job, 42% of the young people in the Unemployed Survey had experienced two or more periods of unemployment. Again, these young people were likelier to be unqualified and as expected tended to be older.

Table 3.1   **Duration of unemployment by age**

Duration	Young People Survey (Nov. 1976)		Unemployed Survey (Jan. 1977)		DE Gazette Jan 1977	
	16/17	18/19	16/17	18/19*	under 18	18/19
	144	106	361	188	122,366	129,962
Up to 3 months	38%	53%	19%	15%	54%	48%
3 – 6 months	33%	20%	27%	29%	23%	24%
6 months – 1 year	23%	16%	43%	27%	20%	19%
1 year and over	6%	11%	11%	28%	3%	9%

*Majority were 18, only 23 were 19 (these young people having had a birthday between first being contacted and being interviewed).

Duration of unemployment by age

Duration	Training Survey (May 1975 – March 1976)			DE Gazette July 1975		
	16/17	18/19	20 – 24	Under 18	18/19	20 – 24
	133	146	306	105,017	127,823	203,386
Up to 3 months	68%	60%	56%	85%	80%	70%
3 – 6 months	18%	15%	17%	10%	12%	15%
6 months – 1 year	8%	18%	13%	4%	7%	10%
1 year and over	5%	6%	14%	0.6%	2%	4%

Unemployment experiences of those now employed or in education

3.20 Some information about the experience of unemployment of those aged 16–19 who were either employed or in education was provided by the Young People Survey. 5% (46) of those in education had been unemployed at some time, as had 36% (663) of those who were employed.

3.21 The majority of the employed who had been unemployed had experienced only one period of unemployment (30% out of the 36% who had been unemployed). Again the increasing difficulties school-leavers, especially those without qualifications, faced in getting jobs in the summer of 1976 are shown by 40% of those who had experienced unemployment having left school in 1976 and 42% having no qualifications.

Job search during unemployment

3.22 Table 3.2 shows the main methods used by the young unemployed to look for jobs. Looking through advertisements in newspapers, visiting the Jobcentre or Employment Office, going to the Careers Office and approaching employers directly were the most frequently mentioned methods. Most 16 and 17 year olds, especially those still looking for their first job, used the Careers Office rather than the Employment Office or Jobcentre (in fact, the Employment Service Agency would usually advise them to); 18 and 19 year olds, on the other hand, were more likely to use the Employment Office or Jobcentre. Noticeably few young people said they were doing nothing, even those who had been unemployed for some time.

3.23 The Unemployed Survey compared methods of job search used at the beginning of the period of unemployment with those used at the time of the survey. Generally there was little change, except for a fall in the numbers using the Careers Office. There was also

Table 3.2 **Job search during recent unemployment**

Method of job finding	Unemployed survey (16-18)		Young People Survey (16-19) Unemployed Section
	At start of unemployment	At time of survey	
Base:	549	473	250
	%	%	%
Newspapers	64	64	60
Careers Office	57	40	45
Employment Office/Jobcentre	54	54	60
Approach employers	56	52	40
Ask friends/acquaintances	24	22	14
Ask parents/relatives	18	17	9
Private employment agency	2	2	6
Other	2	1	12
Nothing	3	7	na
Don't know	—	—	1

a fall in the frequency with which young people were visiting the Careers Office and, to a lesser extent, in the frequency of visits to the Employment Office or Jobcentre. (See table 3.3).

3.24 The fall in usage of the Careers Office occurred among all age groups and was not simply a reflection of young people changing to the Employment Office or Jobcentre as they got older. The main reasons young people gave for going to the Careers Office less frequently were that it did not have many jobs or did not have suitable jobs.

Typical comments were:

"Because there is nothing there. Every time you go, there are loads of you all being sent after one job. You never get a job from them."

"They were not helpful . . they had no jobs left by the time I got there. Mind you, I

Table 3.3 **Unemployed Survey**
Use of the Careers Office and Employment Office

	Users of Careers Office:		Users of Employment Office/Jobcentre:	
	At start of unemployment	At time of survey	At start of unemployment	At time of survey
Sample:	311	190	297	255
Frequency of visit	%	%	%	%
4 days a week or more	8	5	9	6
2 – 3 days a week	14	8	25	19
Once a week	49	46	46	50
Once a fortnight	9	14	4	6
Less often	12	25	5	9
Once only	6	—	3	—
Not stated	2	2	9	10

suppose it's my own fault. I never used to get there until 12 o'clock and all the jobs had gone except for those with 'O' levels and that."

"They try to help you, but they can't get jobs out of thin air for you."

"You get to saying to yourself what's the point in going."

"I'm getting a bit desperate but it's expensive going into Huddersfield 2 or 3 times a week."

"They didn't seem to help me at all. After about a month I stopped going. They never even looked for jobs, didn't tell me I could register for work at the Jobcentre."

3.25 The lower usage of the Careers Office by employers for recruiting to semi- and unskilled jobs is commented on in Chapter 7. Many of the unemployed young people would be looking for jobs at this level. Consequently, the drop in usage of the Careers Offices could be a reflection of a growing awareness by the young people that the Careers Office is less likely to have those sort of vacancies.

Attitudes towards the 'official' services

3.26 Those in the Unemployed Survey were asked for each of the agencies they had used, if they had found the staff at the Careers Office and at the Employment Office or Jobcentre easy to talk to, what help or advice they had been given and how useful they thought the help and advice was. The results are shown in tables 3.4 and 3.5. The majority of those using the Careers Office had found the staff easy to talk to, though this was less true of the Employment Office or Jobcentre. This could be, however, a reflection of the more impersonal methods of job seeking used in the self-service sections of the Jobcentre or Employment Office, eg. looking at cards on boards, or a reflection of a different type of young person using the Careers Office.

3.27 Those using the Careers Office were more likely than those using Employment Offices or Jobcentres to mention definite help or advice they had received. Careers officers were, specifically, more likely to have encouraged the young person to keep trying to find a job. For both agencies, however, there was a drop between the start of unemployment and the time of the survey in mention of help or advice being given, being told about vacancies and being sent after jobs. Among those who were still unemployed (76 out of 549 in the Unemployed Survey had got jobs at the time of interviewing), only one in three of those using the Careers Office and one in five of those using the Employment Office or Jobcentre thought they were getting useful help or advice.

Table 3.4

	Careers Office:		Employment Office/Jobcentre:	
	At start of unemployment	At time of survey	At start of unemployment	At time of survey
Sample: All using at that time	311	190	297	255
People there were:	%	%	%	%
Easy to talk to	85	79	63	56
Not easy to talk to	13	15	31	34
Don't know	2	6	6	10
Opinion of help/advice given:	%	%	%	%
Help/advice given useful	44	36	26	21
Help/advice given not useful	33	29	27	21
No answer on help/advice	2	1	8	9
Not help/advice given	22	35	38	48

Table 3.5 **Unemployed Survey**
Help or advice given at Careers Office or Jobcentre/EO

	Careers Office:		Employment Office/Jobcentre:	
	At start of unemployment	At time of survey	At start of unemployment	At time of survey
Sample: All using at that time	311	190	297	255
Help or advice given	%	%	%	%
Told me of vacancies/sent me after jobs	21	13	13	7
Arranged interviews for me	7	5	5	5
Said they would look out for something suitable	9	10	7	7
Told me to try approaching employers/ looking at papers etc	9	3	2	*
Asked about my interests	7	1	2	2
Advised me to try for a wide range of jobs	2	3	*	1
Advised on types of work to apply for	2	—	2	2
Encouraged me to keep trying	16	21	8	6
Advised further education/training	4	3	1	1
Just looked through their lists/files of jobs	3	3	5	2
Just told me to look at the board	5	4	17	15
Other help or advice	5	3	2	2
Said no jobs were available	5	4	1	2
Gave no specific help or advice	18	30	35	43
Don't know/not stated	4	5	3	5

*Less than 0·5%

Job aspirations

3.28 Young people in the Unemployed Survey were asked if they had a particular type of job they were applying for, with reference to the start of their period of unemployment and the time they were interviewed; 58% said they had been applying for a particular type of job at the start of their period of unemployment. These were more likely to be in the younger age groups, and to be girls rather than boys. For boys, craft occupations were the most frequently mentioned type of job applied for (42% of boys applying for a particular type of job), though only 13% of boys in the sample who had worked before had been employed in craft jobs. Clerical occupations (34%) were most often sought by the girls but only 20% of girls in the sample who had worked before had been employed in clerical jobs.

3.29 The importance employers attached to a good basic standard of education for skilled manual and non-manual jobs is described in Chapter 7. However, many of the unemployed had few or no qualifications. It seems then that some, at least, of these young people were applying for jobs they stood little chance of getting.

Jobs applied for and expectations of getting a job

3.30 Only 8% in the Unemployed Survey had not applied for any jobs; 34% had applied for between 1 and 5 jobs, 24% for between 6 and 10 jobs, 16% for between 11 and 20 jobs and 12% for more than 20 jobs. Very few of the unemployed had been offered a job but turned it down: 7% in the Unemployed Survey and 12% for the unemployed in the Young People Survey. The main reasons given for turning down jobs were poor pay, distance of travel and dislike of the work involved.

3.31 Many of those in the Unemployed Survey had expected to find a job easily at the start of their unemployment (42%) but considerably fewer thought so at the time when they were interviewed (16%). Those who had been unemployed longest were more likely to have been optimistic at the start, probably reflecting the worsening employment situation. Asked why they did not think they would get a job easily, typical comments were:

"Because there is no work. Everyone in this place is looking for work. I know of a lot of people in and around this area who are looking all the time for work."

"It's bad and if you have looked at newspapers and asked your pals and gone looking for jobs – then you know it's no good."

"Walked from Pier Head to Bootle one day asking everyone (factories, shops, etc) if there are any jobs available."

Other activities

3.32 The young people in the Unemployed Survey were asked what, apart from looking for a job, they were doing to keep themselves occupied during their time unemployed.

The main activities mentioned were:

	Boys	Girls
	290	259
	%	%
Helping mum/housework	23	74
Sport/walking/fishing	30	5
Playing records	14	5
General reading	7	13
Seeing/visiting friends and relatives	14	16
No activity mentioned	14	6

Other activities, such as looking after children, decorating, gardening, studying and technical or creative pastimes were also mentioned.

3.33 There were differences one might expect by sex, but little difference by age. Those who had been unemployed for six months or longer were somewhat less likely than others to mention any specific activity (18% of these young people said they had done nothing apart from look for a job). Other studies (3) have shown that long periods of unsuccessful job seeking are liable to lead to depression and a sense of fatalism about being unable to get a job. The effect is often that the individual adopts a life-style consistent with living off benefit and being unemployed, eg. staying in bed late in the morning and reducing social activities while maintaining a minimum level of job-seeking, although often with little hope of getting a job. Until recently, young people were usually only unemployed for short periods. This has now changed, and the increasing lengths of time they spend out of work may be producing similar effects to those that have been observed in adults.

Conclusions

3.34 The extent to which unemployment is concentrated in communities is shown by the evidence that a fifth of the unemployed in the survey were living in families where at least one other member was unemployed and very many more had friends who were unemployed. Some groups of young people also seem to suffer particularly from unemployment. A small but significant number of the young unemployed had special handicaps which would increase their difficulties in getting a job. On a much larger scale, the surveys found that young people with no qualifications were more likely to suffer unemployment. They were also more likely to be unemployed more than once and to spend a longer time unemployed. These findings show a clear need to direct the resources intended to help the unemployed towards certain areas and certain types of young people and to provide programmes which help meet special needs.

3.35 Most of the unemployed were looking hard for jobs and using both the 'official' services and more informal methods to do so. However, some unemployed young people had stopped using the Careers Office, even though they generally thought it more friendly and helpful than the Jobcentre or Employment Office. The main reason for this seems to be that jobs which would suit young people are not being registered with the Careers Office.

3.36 As young people spend longer periods of time unemployed there is evidence to suggest that a number are suffering the psychological effects of long-term unemployment noted in studies of adults. Many were pessimistic of their chances of getting a job and 18% of those who had been unemployed for six months or more said they did nothing to occupy their spare time except look for jobs. Encouragement and aid to restore self-confidence may be necessary to help these young people enter the labour force.

Chapter 4   Youth unemployment – a brief investigation of the causes

Introduction

4.1 The Government and the MSC, in devising ways to help young people, needed to know to what extent youth unemployment was influenced by the general unemployment level and would, therefore, fall as the general picture improved and to what extent it had been worsening steadily irrespective of the general level of unemployment and might, therefore, remain high when employment prospects generally improved.

4.2 The surveys provide some information on the changes that have taken place in recruitment over the last few years; on the factors which employers say have influenced their recruitment policies; and on some of the longer-term trends that have been suggested as causing high youth unemployment. This information, though not in itself conclusive, suggests that youth unemployment contains both a cyclical element, affected by the general level of unemployment, and an element resulting from longer-term trends not directly affected by general unemployment levels.

Changes in the recruitment of young people

4.3 Comparison of the survey data and national statistics indicates that the pattern of industrial and occupational entry to employment by young people has remained relatively stable for several years (4). About a third of young people are employed in manufacturing but significant numbers are employed in construction, distribution (especially girls) and miscellaneous services (see table 8.1). In the past few years overall employment opportunities in these industries have not declined significantly relative to others. There has been some reorganisation in distribution, but that is now largely complete; construction is subject to a distinct cycle which has depressed job opportunities in the last few years; but the services have been a growth area. Within manufacturing, the long-term decline of textile production, where young people account for a larger proportion of total employees than in other industries, may have affected employment opportunities for young people, especially girls.

4.4 Although the pattern of industrial and occupational entry seems to have been relatively stable since 1971, the overall numbers of young people entering employment have declined; partly because more are staying on at school or going on to further and higher education but, more significantly, because of a large rise in unemployment among young people.

How employers decide on recruitment levels for young people

4.5 When asked how they decide on the number of young people to recruit each year, the majority of employers in the survey said they recruited as required for all types of jobs, though 38% of those recruiting young people to skilled manual jobs did so according to fixed numbers, probably reflecting a regular apprentice intake.

4.6 The level of business activity and the replacement of staff who have left were the main reasons given by employers for recruiting as required. The level of business activity had the greatest influence on the recruitment of young people to other manual jobs, especially compared to office or shop jobs where recruitment is more often on a replacement basis, or to skilled manual jobs where there is a greater need to maintain fixed levels of recruitment.

Effect of 1976 conditions on normal recruitment patterns

4.7 About two-thirds of employers said conditions in 1976 had had no effect on recruitment, but of those who said conditions had affected recruitment more than twice as many had recruited less rather than more. No single important reason other than the level of business activity emerged that had affected 1976 recruitment patterns.

Effect on recruitment intentions of an increase or decrease in business

4.8 The findings described above suggest that youth unemployment is part of the general unemployment problem resulting from low levels of business activity. If this were the only factor, however, a revival in business activity could be expected to reduce unemployment amongst young people.

An attempt was made to test this by asking employers which of a number of statements about recruitment would best describe their policy if business/work loads were to increase by 10–15% over the next twelve months. Answers were as follows:

Base: all employers recruiting young people	636
	%
Aim to recruit experienced workers	55
Aim to recruit inexperienced workers of 16-18 years	20
Aim to recruit inexperienced workers regardless of age	10
Aim to recruit other inexperienced workers	7
Others	1
No need to recruit/existing work force could cope	24
Don't know	2

4.9 75% of employers said they would have to recruit more workers; but the majority of firms said they would prefer to recruit experienced workers. Manufacturing (64%), construction (80%) and utilities and transport (63%) showed a greater preference for recruiting experienced workers; finance, business and administration (30%), distribution (27%) and other services (26%) showed a greater willingness to take on inexperienced young people.

4.10 Asked the converse of the previous question: what would they do if work levels fell sufficiently to require a sudden reduction in the work force, nearly half (49%) said they would make compulsory redundancies, either on a 'last in, first out' basis or on ability. Both of these could affect young people disproportionately since they are likely to have been employed for a shorter time than older workers and because their relative lack of experience may be equated with ability.

4.11 Overall, it seems that the level of business activity has influenced the recruitment of young people, particularly to other manual type jobs, but that an upturn in business would not necessarily provide sufficient jobs for young people, many employers saying they would prefer to recruit experienced workers. In the event of a further downturn in business, employers said they would stop recruiting and, in some cases, make redundancies; both of which would be likely to increase youth unemployment.

Longer-term trends

4.12 A number of trends, not directly affected by the level of business activity, have been suggested as contributing to high levels of youth unemployment. For example:

a) technological change may have reduced requirements for semi- or unskilled workers and so reduce job opportunities for young people, especially those with few or no qualifications, who would normally enter such jobs;

b) increasing numbers of working married women may have increased competition for jobs, particularly for semi- and unskilled jobs, to the detriment of young people;

c) young people may be leaving school with abilities and attitudes which do not match those required by employers and so compete poorly with other potential recruits;

d) increased levels of benefit may have affected the efforts young people make to find jobs;

e) reduced pay differentials between young and older workers and a lowering of the age threshold at which young people receive the adult wage may have made young people less attractive to employers.

4.13 The surveys provide some evidence as to whether, and to what extent, these trends have been operating.

Technological change

4.14 Head offices were asked whether technological change had influenced recruitment; very few thought so. Only 3 of the 18 respondents in the head office interviews mentioned it spontaneously as being likely to influence the recruitment of young people. Two of the three were in the public sector, the other in manufacturing. In two sectors – construction and banking – it was felt that technological change had gone almost as far as it could and, therefore, would have only a marginal influence on recruitment. In the retail sector there had been a gradual change away from small units with counter service towards larger units employing the 'cash and wrap' system, but the effect of this was difficult to assess because of mergers and take-overs. In manufacturing and those parts of the public sector concerned with manufacturing, the introduction of technological change was generally regarded as a long-term exercise. Overall, at least in the industries covered by the sample, technological change does not seem to have been an important factor in youth unemployment.

Married women

4.15 The increasing numbers of married women staying on at work or returning to work after raising families may be one reason why young people are finding it harder to get work. Housewives returning to work were considered alongside young people for recruitment for 40% of the non-manual jobs and 38% of the manual jobs employers were asked about. Employers were asked, if applicants of broadly similar qualifications were available, whether young people or another type of recruit was preferred. While 42% did not express a preference, 40% preferred housewives returning to work to young people. Even housewives seeking their first jobs, although as inexperienced as young people, were preferred to young people in the majority of those cases where a preference was stated.

Education

4.16 Education standards come in for some criticism by employers, many of whom felt the attitudes and abilities of young people coming to them for work had declined in recent years and compared unfavourably with those of older applicants. This aspect is discussed in Chapter 7, Recruitment. Many of the unemployed did, in fact, have few or no qualifications and most left school at the earliest possible opportunity. Their job aspirations were often for higher level jobs than they were likely to be able to obtain, possibly because their educational standard and attitude to work would have been regarded as unsatisfactory by employers.

Benefit levels

4.17 It is claimed that rising benefit levels have affected the efforts of the unemployed to get jobs by reducing the financial hardships of unemployment, at least initially. It is difficult to assess the effects on young people, because a number have not been earning before and many are not eligible for unemployment benefit, only for the means-tested social security benefits. In the Unemployed Survey, 54% said they were getting the basic level of social security (£9 per week), 5% less than this and 41% more than this (37% receiving between £11 and £13 per week; the current rate of unemployment benefit being £12.90 per week). For the majority of those who had had jobs previously this was a significant reduction in income (net pay in most recent jobs was less than £15 for only 24%, £16-£20 for 38%, £21-£25 for 15% and more than £26 for 12%). For the unemployed in the Young People Survey, who cover a slightly wider age range, benefit levels were, on average, higher but still below past levels of income earned by those who had previously been employed.

4.18 Evidence also suggests that the majority of the unemployed were looking hard for jobs, and did so even at the start of their unemployment. The surveys gave no evidence that receipt of benefit has an effect on job search for young people.

Pay

4.19 It has been suggested that reduced pay differentials between young people and older workers, partly caused by the 'flat-rate' pay settlements of recent years, and the lowering of the age threshold at which young people receive the adult rate of pay have made employers less willing to employ young people. Whilst the surveys were unable to collect conclusive information on pay differentials – that would have required detailed information about levels of both adult and young people's pay over a number of years – there was some anecdotal evidence in the Employers Survey which suggests the effect of these two aspects may not have been great.

4.20 Those firms who never recruited young people or did not recruit young people in 1976 but had done so in the past did not mention pay as a factor. In fact the levels of pay that unemployed young people reported as having earned previously (see Chapter 8, Young People at Work) suggest that they are still relatively inexpensive to employ.

4.21 82% of those firms who had recruited a young person in 1976 stated that the lowering of the age at which young people receive the full adult rate (reported on average as $19\frac{1}{2}$ years, but for other manual jobs as 18 years) had no effect on recruitment. Only in Scotland did the proportion saying the change had an effect rise significantly to 31%.

Conclusions

4.22 High levels of youth unemployment are part of the general problem of high unemployment caused by the depressed state of the economy. Evidence suggests, however, that an improvement in the level of business activity which would reduce the general level of unemployment, might still leave a relatively high level of youth unemployment; many employers preferring to recruit older workers. Those most vulnerable are young people with few or no qualifications who would traditionally enter semi- or unskilled jobs and who may be faced with considerable competition from other potential recruits, whom employers see as much better prospects.

Chapter 5

Attitudes towards publicly-funded programmes and other forms of help for the young unemployed

Introduction

5.1 Both employers and the young people in the surveys were asked about aspects of current and potential programmes for helping the young unemployed. Employers were asked directly about the existing programmes; their knowledge of, use of and attitude towards them; and what else they think could be done. The questions put to the young people were designed not only to seek attitudes towards existing programmes, but to identify aspects of those programmes which could be improved, to test reactions to new types of help and to find the most attractive combination of elements for programmes.

5.2 The report on Young People and Work (5) describes fully the various programmes for unemployed young people. In brief, the major features were:

a) subsidies to recruit workers – originally the Recruitment Subsidy for School-Leavers (RSSL), now the Youth Employment Subsidy (YES), and subsidies to retain workers rather than make them redundant – the Temporary Employment Subsidy (TES);

b) grants to encourage employers to provide more training – Incentive Training Grants;

c) funding for employers and other organisations to provide temporary work – Job Creation Programme (JCP), Work Experience Programme (WEP);

d) direct training provision – Training Opportunities for young people; and

e) programmes to meet the special needs of some young people – Rehabilitation and Community Industry (CI).

The Employment Transfer Scheme (ETS), which helps unemployed workers to move from the Assisted Areas in order to get a job, is also open to young people.

Employers' knowledge of, use of, and attitude towards programmes

5.3 Employers were asked which government measures to help the unemployed they knew about (both unprompted and then prompted) and which, if any they had taken advantage of. The RSSL was the most well-known (43% mentioned it unprompted, rising to 76% when prompted), and most used scheme (15%). TES was also widely known (31% unprompted rising to 67% when prompted) but used by only a few (7%). JCP and WEP were not so well-known and had been taken advantage of by relatively few, although at that time WEP had only been in operation for a couple of months.

5.4 Larger firms and the textile industry were more likely to have known about and have made use of these measures; in particular, the textile industry had used the TES (34%). The finance, business services and administration sector (which includes local authorities) was well informed about JCP and WEP: 55% of employers in this sector knew about JCP and 44% about WEP. In fact JCP was most used by local authorities (45% had used it). A few employers had seriously considered using various measures but had not done so, usually because the company was not eligible or because there was no suitable candidate available, though some criticised restrictions in, or even the concept of, the schemes.

5.5 Head office views of government measures were rather more critical. They complained of there being too many schemes which were badly publicised and changed too frequently so that it was difficult for organisations to keep track of what was applicable to them. They also criticised the temporary nature of many of the schemes which meant, in the words of one employer, "All we are doing is to train people for unemployment again." In general, they thought the Government should be addressing itself to the question of how to reduce unemployment through measures to help economic recovery.

5.6 Of those programmes specifically for unemployed young people, WEP was the most favourably regarded. A number of organisations already operated what they described as 'mini-WEPs', in which pupils from local schools spent short periods working in the organisations and learning about working life. It was this aspect, bridging the information gap between young people and work, that employers thought particularly useful.

Employers' ideas about other schemes and remedies for youth unemployment

5.7 Having already discussed the existing schemes, employers were asked whether they could suggest any sort of scheme or change in circumstances (other than an upturn in business) which would encourage them to recruit more young people: 78% said no. The remainder mentioned the following:

	Number of mentions
Education	34
Training	33
Incentives	16
Changes within own establishment	10
Legislation	9
Mobility of existing work force	9
Policy/attitudes of top management or head office	7
Attitude of unions	6
Earlier retirements	5
Costs of work force	4
Others	13

5.8 Those mentioning education would take on more young people if applicants of a suitable calibre were available (13 mentions). Others thought young people's education should be more work-orientated (11 mentions), that educational standards should be generally improved (5 mentions) and that there should be more liaison with schools (3 mentions). The main items mentioned under training were more money (15 mentions), the introduction of their own training or apprenticeship scheme (5 mentions) and increasing or improving their own training or apprenticeship scheme (5 mentions). Main comments about incentives were that they should be retained or increased (5 mentions), extend to those ineligible at present (5 mentions) or that other incentives should be created (3 mentions). Head offices generally made suggestions similar to these.

5.9 Head offices were asked where they thought the remedy for youth unemployment lay – with the young people themselves, with the Government, with the education system or in their own hands. The majority placed the main responsibility on the Government. They felt any improvement in employment required the Government to place the economy on a proper footing. Some felt young people, as individuals, could do more to help themselves; others suggested various measures such as better vocation preparation for young people at school, a shorter working week, early retirement, paying employment premiums for the recruitment of young people, giving special assistance to immigrant children and channelling recruitment schemes through Industrial Training Boards.

Unemployed young people - attitudes towards help

5.10 The majority of unemployed young people in the surveys thought there was not enough done to help people like themselves (60% of the unemployed in the Young People Survey and 61% in the Unemployed Survey). They thought both central and local government, employers, careers offices, Jobcentres, Employment Offices, schools and teachers should all be doing more to help them. The main suggestions for the ways these organisations could help were that central and local government should create jobs; employers should provide more work-sharing and training schemes and should pay less attention to qualifications when hiring people; the job finding agencies should give more personal attention and make more of an effort to find jobs for people; and schools and teachers should do more to train young people at school for entering work and give them advice about training.

5.11 To test the extent to which there is a demand among young unemployed people for certain types of help they were asked about four kinds of opportunity: the opportunity to go back to school or to go on to college; the opportunity for a desired form of training; the opportunity to undertake community service; and the opportunity to move in order to get a job.

Going back to school or on to college

5.12 Most of the young people in the Unemployed Survey had left school at the earliest possible opportunity and said they had wanted to do so. Despite this, 41% said they sometimes wished they had stayed at school longer and one in four (24%) had seriously thought of going back to school or to college to get extra qualifications, though these were more likely to be those already with some qualifications. 30% of those with at least some CSE passes said they had seriously thought of going back compared with only 17% of those with no qualifications. Girls (who tended to have somewhat better qualifications than boys) were more likely to have seriously considered returning to school or to college (30% of girls compared with 18% of boys).

5.13 Very few, 3% (16), had gone back or had definite plans to go back. Among those who had given it serious thought but had not acted, the main inhibiting factors mentioned were lack of knowledge of how to go about it or reasons of finance.

5.14 In the Unemployed Survey 40% of all those interviewed and 84% of those who had seriously considered going back to school or on to college said they would take the chance to go back to school or on to college if it were offered to them. Those who already had some qualifications showed more interest (64% of the unqualified would not take the chance to return); 46% of those not prepared to go back to school did not know why; other reasons for not being prepared to return were dislike of school or college (21%), the desire to have a job (10%), past failure at school (6%), and financial reasons (4%). Typical replies were:—

"Well, I did not care for school when I was there and I doubt if I could concentrate now."

"I was always unhappy at learning."

"Even if you get qualifications you still can't get a job."

"I just want to have a job, have some cash in my pocket."

5.15 Rather more of the unemployed in the Young People Survey had seriously thought about going back to school or on to college (36%) and were prepared to go back to school or to college if offered the chance (57% overall, but only 49% of 16 year olds and 53% of those with no qualifications). Since many of the unemployed sample came from inner city areas where young people may be more alienated from the schools, it is probable that the Young People Survey sample, though much smaller, is more indicative of the national picture.

Undertaking a training or non-educational qualification

5.16 Young people in the Unemployed Survey were asked if there was any sort of training or qualification that they wished they had. Two in five (40%) said there was. Boys were more likely to want some sort of training or qualification than girls (44% of boys compared with 36% of girls).

5.17 Among boys who wanted a particular training or qualification, 23% wanted apprenticeships and 55% some other vocational or skill training. Girls wanted shorthand and typing (33%), vocational or skill training (28%) and nursing (15%). Fewer than two in five of those who wished they had a particular qualification or training thought they had ever had the chance to get it, but 90% would take the chance if it were offered to them.

Community service

5.18 Reactions to a possible national programme of community service work were obtained from a question asking the unemployed if they were willing to spend 6 months to 1 year doing community work (eg taking care of children, doing outdoor work or helping old and disabled people) while being paid at unemployment benefit level (£12.90 per week at that time).

5.19 The mention of specific types of work may have had some influence on replies, e.g. many girls said they were willing to take part because they liked looking after children and allowance should, perhaps, be made for this. Many of the unemployed, especially girls and younger respondents were willing, however, to take part in such a scheme; some 69% of girls and 43% of boys in the Unemployed Survey.

5.20 Those in the Unemployed Survey who were not willing to take part were asked why this was so: the main reasons given were the rate of pay (44%) and the types of work (28%). It seems a further 20% of the sample might be persuaded to take part if the remuneration was higher although they generally wanted a much higher rate of pay – over £20 per week in most cases.

5.21 The main reasons young people gave for being interested were that it would give them something to do and that they would be doing something useful and of help to the community. When asked whether they thought the scheme should be made compulsory 53% of those in the Unemployed Survey thought it would be a very or fairly good idea compared with only 38% of the unemployed in the Young People Survey.

Moving to get a job

5.22 Unemployed young people were asked if they would be prepared to move if a job were offered to them in another part of the country: 49% of those in the Young People Survey said they would; as did 45% of those in the Unemployed Survey.

5.23 Boys were more willing to move than girls. Slightly more of the 18 and 19 year olds than the 16 and 17 year olds were willing. The most common reasons young people gave for not being prepared to move were:

	Unemployed Survey	Unemployed in Young People Survey
Base:	239	127
	%	%
Want to stay with family/Don't want to leave home	48	50
Like home town/want to stay in this area	18	20
Want to stay with friends/people I know	17	11
Now married/personal reasons	n.a.	16

5.24 It would seem that for all four types of help there is an unmet demand, although the hypothetical nature of these questions must be taken into account.

Young people's reactions to elements of programmes

5.25 Reactions to elements of various existing and potential training and work experience schemes were tested by a question which asked those in the Young People Survey and in the Unemployed Survey to consider eleven elements which were descriptions of aspects of various existing or possible schemes to help young people. The young people were asked to rate the elements on a five point scale from 'very important to me' to 'not at all important to me', in the context of their present situation.

Table 5.1 **Ranking of elements of existing and potential training and work experience schemes**

"The Government has recently been trying to find ways of helping young people who have not been able to find jobs or would like to change jobs by providing schemes for temporary work or training. I am going to read out some features of these schemes. For each feature I read out I want you to tell me how important or unimportant it is to you in your present situation."

	Young People Survey				Unemployed Survey	
	Employed		Unemployed		Unemployed	
	and never unemployed	and has been unemployed	and has worked	and has never worked	and has worked	and has never worked
Base	1115	645	147	103	355	214
The chance to learn the basic skills for a job that you're already decided on	2	3	1	1	1	1
The chance to learn a skill *on the job*	3	2	3	4	3	4
The chance to work with a supervisor who tries to understand you and doesn't expect you to know everything straightaway	1	1	2	3	2	3
The chance to get a certificate or recommendation	4	5	5	5	5	5
The chance to learn how to make a good impression on an employer	5	4	4	2	4	2
The chance to try out different kinds of work	6	6	6	7	6	6
The chance to learn a skill *in a special centre*	7	7	7	6	7	6
The chance to do something useful for the community	8	8	8	7	8	8
The chance to leave whenever you like	9	9	10	11	10	11
The chance to work for a local employer	10	10	9	9	9	9
The chance to work in a small group	11	11	11	10	11	10

5.26 The elements are shown at the side of Table 5.1 with the ranking of each element by six sub-samples from the two surveys. The ranking was derived from simple numerical weighting of the points of the scale, and in terms of absolute scores the elements fall roughly into three bands as indicated by the heavy horizontal lines in the table. The top band were those elements rated between 'fairly important' and 'very important'. The middle band were grouped around the 'fairly important' level while the bottom band were rated between the 'doesn't matter' and the bottom of the 'fairly important' scores.

5.27 The overall ranking of the features is remarkably consistent although there are slight differences. The features most widely seen as important by the unemployed were the opportunities:

a) to learn the basic skills for a job they have already decided on;

b) to learn a skill *on the job;*

c) to work with a supervisor who tries to understand them;

d) to learn how to make a good impression on an employer; and

e) to gain a certificate or recommendation.

5.28 There is a consensus among the unemployed that the opportunity to learn the basic skills for a job they have already decided on is most important. Those who had never worked before rated as second in importance the opportunity to learn how to make a good impression on an employer, while those who had worked before rated second the opportunity to work with a supervisor who tries to understand them. This difference probably reflects the desire of those who have never worked to 'get a foot on the ladder' while those who had been in employment would know from experience the importance of sympathetic supervision. The latter interpretation is supported by the high ranking those employed gave to this element.

5.29 The rating of the two methods of acquiring skill training is also of interest since the consistent difference of three or four ranks between the 'on the job' and the 'special centre' training probably reflects the desire of young people to learn in a practical context and, possibly, to avoid the formal training atmosphere which may be associated with school.

5.30 Young people were asked what they thought was a fair take-home wage per week for them to be paid on a government training scheme. The average figure quoted by each age group in the surveys was:

	16	17	18	19
Young People Survey	£19.00	£19.60	£21.60	£23.30
Unemployed Survey	£17.12	£19.04	£25.10*	

*The Unemployed Survey contained a few young people who had become 19 between being contacted and being interviewed.

16–18 year olds on the new Programme of Opportunities for Young People will, in most cases, be paid an allowance of £18 a week plus discretionary payments for travelling costs above £2 – a figure very close to the average that young people told us they thought was fair.

Conclusions

5.31 Subsidies for employing workers were the most widely known and most used Government measures to help the unemployed. Generally the measures current at the time of interviewing were not well regarded by employers. Many thought the schemes were too numerous, badly publicised and changing too frequently. The new programme of opportunities for young people will replace the variety of temporary measures with a coherent and consistent scheme.

5.32 Most unemployed young people thought that not enough was being done to help them. Many, over half in some cases, said they were willing to take up opportunities such as returning to school or going on to college, training for a skill they wanted, taking part in community service, or moving home for a job. Others showed a marked reluctance to take up such offers of help, sometimes for financial or social reasons, for example not being paid sufficient or not wanting to leave family or friends; but sometimes for reasons which indicate an alienation from 'official' schemes and the institutions they involved, for example dislike of school or college. A less 'formal' approach may be necessary for helping these young people.

5.33 Unemployed young people were remarkably consistent when asked to rate in order of importance elements of training and work experience schemes. They rated as most important three elements which would help them find jobs – the opportunity to learn the basic skills for a job, to learn how to make a good impression on an employer and to get a certificate or recommendation – and two elements describing conditions on schemes – the opportunity to learn *on the job* and with a sympathetic supervisor. The new programme of opportunities for young people takes account of these needs.

PART II

From school to work

Education and the preparation of young people for work

Introduction

6.1 The transition of young people between school and work has, for some time, been the subject of much discussion, debate and research. In particular, concern has focused on the role of education and the job advice and placing services in preparing the young person for work and smoothing the transition. The surveys provide evidence on these issues which adds to and up-dates the information already available from other studies, and clarifies some of the current arguments.

Young people at school and in full-time education and training

6.2 This section refers to those young people still in full-time education or training: the courses they are doing and their reasons for doing them; their experience of employment and unemployment; and the ease with which they think they will be able to get a job when they leave.

6.3 The Young People Survey interviewed 997 young people who were in full-time education or training which was not paid for by an employer. The majority of these (74%) were at school or sixth form college, 21% were at colleges of further education (CFEs) or technical colleges, 2% at Skillcentres or other training centres and 2% at other colleges.

6.4 18 and 19 year olds were more likely to be at CFEs or technical colleges and 16 and 17 year olds to be at school. Girls were more likely to be attending CFEs than boys (26% compared with 16%), and less likely to be at school (69% compared with 79%). This could be because more boys intended to go on to higher education than did girls – 'to go on to further/higher education' was given by 45% of boys but only 39% of girls as the reason for doing the course for which they were studying.

6.5 The type of establishment attended varied also according to level of educational attainment. Those with GCE 'O' level or CSE grade 1, and especially with 5 or more 'O' levels or equivalent, were more likely to be at school and less likely to be at college than those with fewer qualifications. They were also more likely to expect to continue in education for more than three years. This is probably because school is the natural route for the better qualified young person who intends to go on to higher education while the vocational emphasis of CFEs is more relevant for those with fewer qualifications who do not expect to go on to higher education.

6.6 The vast majority of young people in education were aiming to pass an examination at the end of their course, usually for an academic qualification. However, as many as perhaps 14% of young people without qualifications were not entering for examinations. This compares with recent Department of Education and Science and Scottish Education Department figures for 1976 indicating that 17% of school leavers had not been entered for or did not sit public examinations, representing some 134,000 young people who entered the labour market from school without having even attempted a public examination. (6)

Reasons for course selection

6.7 When asked the reasons for doing the course upon which they were currently engaged, young people gave as the main reasons: to go on to further or higher education (42%), to improve their chances of getting a job (40%) and to meet the requirements of a technical or professional body (13%).

6.8 The desire to go on to further or higher education was mentioned most frequently by those with 5 or more 'O' levels or equivalent (61%) who made less frequent mention of the need to improve their chances of getting a job. The desire to improve the chance of getting a job was most frequently reported by those with only CSE grades below

hese results are consistent with the pattern already mentioned i.e.
ied young people tend to move into a vocational stream of education
1 the job, and specific qualifications necessary for it, are paramount:
ied the possibility of higher education probably makes the question of
1ote.

6.9 Those with no qualifications, largely 16 year olds in their 5th year at school, gave as the main reasons for doing the course that it could improve the chances of getting a job (44%), that they were too young to leave school (32%) and that they wanted to go on to further/higher education (29%). The 32% who said they were too young to leave school may be an indication of those, least motivated towards school, who are there only, or largely, because of the legal requirement.

Past experience of employment and unemployment

6.10 A small minority (37 or 4%) in full-time education or training had been employed full-time other than in holiday jobs, and a similarly small minority (46 or 5%), somewhat overlapping those who had had work, had experienced unemployment.

6.11 Of the 68 young people who had returned to full-time education or gone on to full-time training after employment, unemployment or both, most said that they had begun studying again because they wanted to get a better or more interesting job and thought qualifications would help in this. About a fifth said they were unable to get a job. Two-thirds had gone to college and 16% to a Skillcentre or other training centre; only 18% had returned to school. This is consistent with the vocational rather than academic reasons which many of them gave for returning.

Ease of finding jobs

6.12 Over half (56%) of all those in full-time education or training thought it would be very or fairly difficult for them to get a job when they left. Only 35% thought it would be very or fairly easy; 10% did not know. Those with no qualifications, those expecting to leave in 1977 and the 16 year olds were all more pessimistic (68%, 65% and 61% respectively thought it would be very or fairly difficult for them to get a job). The reasons young people gave for their pessimism were: that jobs generally were scarce, that the type of work they wanted was scarce and that many other young people with at least as many or more qualifications as themselves would also be looking for work.

Influence of school experience on subsequent employment

6.13 Three factors were considered which may have affected the subsequent ability to find jobs of those who had left school. These factors were experience of work whilst at school, truancy, and illness at school.

Work experience at school

6.14 All young people in the Young People Survey and the Unemployed Survey were asked whether, while at school, they had had any experience of part-time or holiday work, or work experience arranged by the school, or had undertaken voluntary community work. The responses are set out in Table 6.1. It is notable that the unemployed in both surveys had had significantly less experience of part-time or holiday work than had those who were in full-time employment or in education. (This was not due to age differences between the sub-sets; even among the 16 year olds the unemployed had had considerably less experience of part-time or holiday work). Furthermore those unemployed young people who had worked at some time were much more likely to have undertaken part-time work whilst at school than were those who had never worked. This could reflect the value of work experience whilst at school in helping young people to find and settle down in work, or it could reflect simply the fact that some young

Table 6.1   **Experience of work whilst at school**

	Young People Survey (16 – 19)			Unemployed Survey (16 – 18)		
	In full-time education	In employment	Unemployed	All respondents	No work since leaving school	Worked since leaving school
Part-time or vacation work	68%	63%	43%	39%	30%	49%
Work-experience arranged by the school	10%	12%	12%	14%	11%	18%
Community work	27%	20%	22%	24%	24%	23%

people are more likely, both at school and after school, to be able to find work, because of either their attitudes and abilities or greater local employment opportunities.

6.15 Nearly half (49%) of those now employed who had had either a part-time job, work experience or voluntary work experience whilst at school thought the experience had been useful to them when they started work or while they were working. The main reasons given for this were that the experience had been relevant for their present job and had, in some cases, led directly to a job (33% of those who had had such experience); that it had helped them get on with and get used to meeting other people (50%); and that it had given them an idea of what work was like (19%).

6.16 It seems that, at least for some young people, work experience prior to leaving school does help to smooth the entry to work, though getting the experience is, in most cases, left up to the individual.

Truancy

6.17 Nearly half (46%) of the young people in the Unemployed Survey said they had stayed away from school, other than for reasons of illness, during their last two or three years; 17% had stayed away once or twice, and 29% more often. The latter were more likely to be boys than girls (34% compared with 23%).

6.18 The National Child Development Study (NCDS) sought similar information and found 52% of young people had stayed away from school at some time during their last year at school; and that teachers, when asked about the children, said that the description 'truant' applied 'somewhat' to 12% and 'certainly' to 8% (7).

6.19 Comparison of the findings of the Unemployed Survey with those of the NCDS, although the sources for the information were rather different, suggests that there may be little difference between the unemployed and all young people as to whether they have ever taken time off, but that the unemployed are likely to be truant more frequently. This could contribute towards their subsequent difficulties in getting a job, and other studies have shown a strong correlation between truancy and early employment difficulties (8). However, the unemployed sample showed no difference between those who had played truant and those who had not, in terms of the amount of time they had subsequently worked.

Prolonged illness at school

6.20 Just under one in four (24%) in the Unemployed Survey said that they had been off school ill for a month or more at a time: 11% had had two or more such periods of illness and the evidence does suggest a relationship between long absences from school and subsequent work history, as the following figures show:

Total absences from school through illness (Unemployed Survey)

	3 months or more	less than 3 months
Base:	64	485
Amount of time worked since school:	%	%
none	55	37
some	45	62
unclassifiable	—	1

Attitudes towards work of those in education

6.21 The attitudes young people develop about work while in education may influence their ability to find and settle in work when they leave. To examine their expectations about work, those still in education were asked what things were important to them in a job.

6.22 55% of the young people currently in full-time education mentioned job satisfaction as the most important factor while only 9% felt that good pay was most important. Asked to identify several things important to them in a job, good money was frequently mentioned but still less frequently than job satisfaction. These findings are similar to those found in the NCDS where young people said that the most important aspects of a job were that it should have variety and be well paid (9).

6.23 It may be that the concern and expectation of some school- and college-leavers that work should be interesting and varied causes conflicts when they are faced with what may be dull and routine tasks in a job. This could be a factor in what employers describe as a poor attitude towards work on the part of young people and could be a cause of more frequent job changing among young people.

Advisers and their role in the transition from education to work

6.24 The last few years at school or college are likely to be an important period for the young person in forming his or her ideas about work and about the type of job he or she wants. The role of those advising young people about jobs can be crucial at this time. To assess the extent to which young people are making up their minds about jobs and the importance of help and advice during this period, the surveys asked young people in education if they had changed their minds during the last two years about the type of job they wanted to do and, if so, why. All young people were asked if they had received help and advice from careers teachers, careers officers and parents and how useful they thought the advice had been.

Changing ideas about work

6.25 45% of those who were still in education had changed their ideas during the last two years about the type of work they wanted to do. The reasons given for this were that their ideas had changed as they grew older (27%); that they had found better information (15%); that they had received better advice (10%); or that the job they wanted had become more difficult to get (12%). These findings suggest that the last years in education are an important period for young people in forming ideas about jobs and that help and advice during that period could have an effect on ideas.

Advisers

6.26 Table 6.2 shows the help and advice young people received from careers teachers, careers officers and parents and how useful they found this advice. (The questions asked in each of the surveys were slightly different but the answers are broadly comparable.)

Table 6.2 **Unemployed Survey: help or advice received whilst at school** (16-18 yrs)
Young People Survey: help or advice received ever (16-19 yrs)

	% of sample receiving help	% of those receiving help who thought it useful at time	% of those receiving help who think it useful now
Unemployed Survey (sample = 549)			
Help or advice from careers teacher	53	67	49
Help or advice from careers officer	50	70	56
Help or advice from parents	68	82	82
Employed in Young People Survey (1,778)			
Help or advice from careers teacher	57	61	na
Help or advice from careers officer	60	66	na
Help or advice from parents	59	64	na
Those in education in Young People Survey (997)			
Help or advice from careers teacher	50	72	na
Help or advice from careers officer	37	70	na
Help or advice from parents	43	59	na

6.27 Just over half the young people said they had received help and advice from a careers teacher and most had found it helpful at the time. In the Unemployed Survey, later school leavers were more likely to have received advice from a careers teacher than were earlier leavers; and later leavers and those who had spent more time in work than unemployed were more likely to say the advice was useful. Not surprisingly, only 49% of the unemployed said that the advice was still of use to them although 67% had thought the advice useful when it was given.

6.28 50% of the unemployed young people said they had received advice from a careers officer whilst at school; 60% of employed young people and 37% of those in education said they had, at some time, received advice from a careers officer. These figures seem rather low when compared with Careers Service statistics and it may be that some young people did not remember being given or were not aware they had received advice from a careers officer. Again the majority said they found the advice useful. In the Unemployed Survey rather fewer said they now thought the advice useful than had thought so at the time (56% compared with 70%).

6.29 Parents were as much a source of job advice as were careers teachers and careers officers. The unemployed were more likely to have mentioned receiving help and advice from parents than were those young people in employment or still in education. Also more of the unemployed said they had received help or advice from a parent than said they received help or advice from a careers teacher or careers officer. Generally young people said the help and advice they had received from parents was useful, and this was particularly true of the unemployed, who thought also that the advice was still useful.

6.30 Several other studies have stressed the role of parents in providing vocational guidance for the young person (10). Other studies have confirmed the findings about the advice young people receive from careers teachers. They show that despite most schools having a careers teacher (11) and the majority of young people being aware of such a teacher, many young people claim not to have received personal help from the careers teacher and are generally critical of the range and depth of the guidance given (12).

6.31 The present surveys suggest that not all young people get, or are aware that they get, help and advice from the advice and guidance services whilst at school. They also indicate that some young people, in particular the unemployed, place greater emphasis on the advice they receive from parents.

Employers' opinions of school and the preparation of young people for work

6.32 The Employers Survey was concerned, among other things, with the attitudes which employers held towards the education system and the preparation for work given to young people. Employers were asked if they thought young people applying to them for jobs were well briefed about the jobs, about the firm and about how to behave in an interview. In less-structured interviews with head offices, employers were asked generally about their views on the connections between school and work.

6.33 Two-thirds of the employers felt young people were not well briefed about the job, the firm or how to behave in an interview. Manufacturing firms, especially those in the process and textile industries, stood out as being more critical than average. Responsibility for briefing young people about how to behave in an interview was placed on the school, careers officer and, to a lesser extent, the parents. Employers did think they had a responsibility for briefing young people about the job, and took the main responsibility for briefing the young person about the firm, though in both cases the careers officer was also expected to take some responsibility.

6.34 Employers drew some distinction between applicants for different types of jobs. They expected the school and careers officer to take more responsibility for briefing skilled manual recruits than other manual or non-manual recruits for whom they were prepared to take more responsibility. This could be because they felt that the skilled manual jobs were less specific to one firm than were the other two grades.

6.35 Less-structured interviews carried out at head offices as a part of the Employers Survey revealed considerable concern with the general nature of the relationship between school and work. Employers felt schools regarded industry as 'second best' and that the general tenor of education was too academic. They were concerned over what they thought was too low a priority given to careers education and they wanted young people to be given more information about work and the meaning of 'earning a living'.

6.36 There was considerable willingness on the part of firms to co-operate with schools in this respect although they believed that the education system needed to show more enthusiasm and they recognised that many prejudices, on both sides, had to be overcome before such co-operation could be effectively pursued.

Conclusions

6.37 The findings show that young people who had experienced work whilst at school had generally found it helpful in getting a job or when they were working. However most of these young people had found such experience themselves – few had been provided with work experience by the school. The surveys suggest that more could usefully be done to provide work experience.

6.38 The last few years at school are a time when young people form their ideas about jobs and when information and advice can be an important influence. Many young people received advice from careers teachers, careers officers and parents, and said that they had found it useful. The evidence suggests, however, that some young people, in particular those unemployed in the surveys, placed more importance on the advice they received from their parents, perhaps because of a distrust of official sources.

6.39 Employers were generally critical of the preparation young people had had for presenting themselves for jobs. They were critical also of the links between education and work. In both cases they recognised that industry had a role to play alongside schools, teachers and careers officers.

Chapter 7

Recruitment

Introduction

7.1 For some time there has been concern about the problems facing young people in entering employment and this has been heightened in recent years by the increasing numbers of unemployed young people, especially unemployed school-leavers. Attention has focused on the attitudes and practices of employers towards young recruits and on the role of the job-finding agencies in meeting the needs of their clients. The surveys suggest that some employers are critical of the attitudes and abilities of young applicants and would prefer to recruit from other groups of workers. They suggest, also, that many jobs which would be suitable for young people are not registered with the Careers Service, although this was the most important single source of jobs for young people.

Employers' attitudes towards young people as recruits

7.2 Information from the Employers Survey indicates that young people compete alongside people of all ages for the majority of jobs for which they are eligible. Only apprenticeships are the preserve of young people alone. Consequently, the surveys sought information on the criteria by which employers select recruits and how they think young people compare against other applicants on these criteria.

7.3 Table 7.1 shows the characteristics employers thought essential or desirable in recruits of any age. Willingness and attitude to work was thought most important. The '3Rs' were also important for non-manual and skilled manual jobs but of much less importance for other manual jobs. Employers were, in general, less demanding of recruits for other manual jobs.

7.4 Larger firms tended to be more demanding in terms of basic education and qualifications desired, perhaps because their recruitment procedures are often more formal. Not surprisingly, willingness, appearance and ability to communicate verbally were particularly important for jobs in shops and other services.

Table 7.1

Employers Survey
Essential and desirable characteristics of all recruits

	Those stating essential				Those stating essential or desirable			
	All grades	Skilled manual	Other manual	Non-manual	All grades	Skilled manual	Other manual	Non-manual
Base: those discussing each grade of job	636	183	180	269	636	183	180	269
	%	%	%	%	%	%	%	%
Willingness/attitude to work	76	80	81	70	93	95	94	92
Basic 3Rs	50	52	21	67	74	80	54	83
Good level of numeracy	39	40	13	55	61	62	34	79
Good level of general physical fitness	39	50	47	27	68	75	79	56
Appearance/tidiness	38	29	39	45	76	66	66	89
Good written English/literate	36	21	6	67	61	55	24	90
Ability to communicate well verbally	30	18	18	45	67	63	45	84
Mature/stable	24	30	20	23	54	56	48	55
Specific educational qualifications	23	21	2	38	43	39	10	68
Specific physical attributes (sight, strength, height, etc)	21	27	36	7	44	52	57	29
Willingness to join union	15	22	16	9	23	32	26	14
Past experience	10	19	7	5	38	42	42	33
Existing union membership	5	9	4	2	8	13	11	3
Average no. of attributes mentioned:	4.1	4.2	3.1	4.6	7.1	7.3	5.9	7.7

Table 7.2

Employers Survey

Essential and desirable characteristics: young people compared with other recruits

	% stating attribute essential to all recruits	Net rating* of young people v. older recruits	% thinking young people no different or non-comparable
Willingness/attitude to work	76	−32	46
Basic '3Rs'	50	−34	46
Good level of numeracy	39	−34	50
Good level of general physical fitness	39	+18	70
Appearance/tidiness	38	−28	60
Good written English/literate	36	−42	40
Ability to communicate well verbally	30	−25	53
Mature/stable	24	−50	40
Specific educational qualifications	23	+5	49
Specific physical attributes	21	+16	72
Willingness to join union	15	+5	89
Past experience	10	−57	39
Existing union membership	5	−7	85

*Calculated by subtracting the % of respondents who thought young people were worse on each attribute from the percentage thinking they were better.

The right-hand column on the above table shows the proportion of respondents who felt that young people were no different from older recruits for the job under discussion, or that it was impossible to compare the two.

7.5 Table 7.2 shows how employers rated young people against older recruits on the attributes they thought essential or desirable. Though considerable numbers (over half for several of the attributes) thought young people were no different or could not be compared, those employers that did express a preference were more likely to think young people compared unfavourably with older recruits.

Reasons for refusing young people and preferences for other recruits

7.6 Further indications of employers' views of young people came from the reasons employers gave for refusing job applications from young people and from their preferences for recruiting from other sources.

7.7 The most frequently quoted reasons for refusing job applications from young people were related to attitude and personality (45%), appearance and manners (27%) and lack of basic education (24%). Typical remarks were:

"Untidiness and their general attitude. If they are not polite and have this couldn't-careless attitude when they come for interview I just can't be bothered with them. Some of them don't even bother to talk properly."

"Lack of enthusiasm: one detects a certain feeling that they are only half wanting the job. One also feels that with low retail wages they would prefer to be on the dole."

"The most common one is general appearance and attitude during the interview. I have them coming in with dirty fingernails, untidy hair, tatty dress, which shows what their general attitude to work would be."

"Poor educational standards, unable to fill in a test form. Poor general appearance."

7.8 Employers were asked about their preferences for a number of alternatives to young people as sources of recruits, such as upgrading existing employees or recruiting from other firms, the unemployment register, Training Opportunities Scheme trainees, housewives returning to work and other first-job seekers. Whilst a little over a third of employers thought there was no difference, those employers who did state a preference were, in almost all cases, more likely to prefer other recruits to young people. This was especially true when young people were compared to upgraded existing employees, those recruited from other firms or women returning to work.

Changes in the calibre of young recruits

7.9 Employers were asked whether they thought the calibre of those young people coming to them for jobs had improved or declined in the last five years. Only 21% said they thought there had been an improvement in the calibre of young applicants, 31% thought there had been a decline and 43% that there had been no change. Employers were most critical of applicants for skilled manual jobs: 37% thought the calibre of young people applying for these jobs had declined.

7.10 Asked whether the increased numbers of young people looking for jobs at the time had influenced their answers, the majority of those who felt the calibre of young people had increased thought this was due to increased numbers of young people being available, whereas the majority who felt the calibre had declined did not feel numbers were an influence.

7.11 When pressed for examples of specific areas of improvement or deterioration in young people's abilities, 46% could see no improvement while only 28% had seen no decline. Areas of improvement were in maturity and independence while a decline was noted in attitude to work, the '3Rs', dress and manners.

7.12 The evidence from employers points to a gap between the standards employers say they are looking for in recruits and those they perceive in some of the young applicants coming to them for jobs. They are likely to regard older workers more favourably and to prefer them as recruits.

Employers' recruitment methods

7.13 Employers were asked which methods they used to attract applicants for jobs which they wished to fill; they were asked this in relation to recruits of all ages and in relation to recruiting young people. (The findings are shown in table 7.3.)

7.14 The most important recruitment methods employers used to fill skilled manual and non-manual vacancies were press advertisements (mentioned by 38%), followed by the Jobcentre or Employment Office (mentioned by 25% in respect of skilled manual jobs and 18% in respect of non-manual jobs). For other manual jobs however, press advertisements were much less significant than reference to the Jobcentre which was by far the most important source. The Careers Office was little used, particularly for other manual jobs, which suggests employers may not be registering many jobs (e.g. craftsman's mate, machine operator, etc) which would be suitable for young people.

7.15 The Careers Office was, however, the most common method used by employers to recruit young people to skilled manual and non-manual jobs, while an additional source of recruits to skilled manual jobs was staff introductions of friends and relations: a tradition of skilled men 'speaking up' for their relatives has been commented on in other studies (13). For recruitment to other manual jobs use of the Careers Office was equalled by the more informal method of staff introduction.

Table 7.3

Employers Survey

Most important recruitment method - all ages

	Skilled manual	Other manual	Non-manual
Base: all with each grade	461	502	582
	%	%	%
Jobcentre, Employment Office	25	42	18
Careers Office	5	2	7
Ads – local	37	28	38
– national	5	1	3
Commercial agency	2	1	15
Back files	3	4	3
Upgrade	10	5	7
Transfers	2	2	3
Other	10	13	6

Methods of recruiting young people

	Grades			
	All grades	Skilled manual	Other manual	Non-manual
Base: all recruiting young people	636	183	180	269
	%	%	%	%
Notify Careers Officer	64	71	55	66
Existing staff introduce relations or friends	46	52	56	37
Visit schools and describe firm and job available	30	38	18	33
Arrange visits to firm by young people	28	34	24	27
Refer to files of previous applicants	26	21	23	33
Notify Jobcentres/Employment Offices	25	20	23	29
Local publicity aimed at young people	8	10	5	9
Advertise in local press	1	1	—	—
All others	22	24	18	23
Average no of methods mentioned	2.5	2.7	2.2	2.6

7.16 Asked about their selection methods when recruiting young people, 80% of employers mentioned interviewing, 70% asked for references and 69% put the young person on probation to assess their suitability. Recruits to skilled manual jobs were also likely to be given a written aptitude test (53% of employers said they did so). In general, selection for both skilled manual and non-manual jobs was more rigorous than for other manual jobs.

7.17 The overall picture that emerges is that of employers taking more trouble in recruiting to skilled manual jobs and non-manual jobs than to other manual jobs. These differences probably result from the greater investment that the former groups of workers represent to the employer which makes him willing to take more trouble and spend more money on their recruitment. It does perhaps suggest, however, that the onus is placed on the young person looking for other manual jobs to do more to find a job.

Table 7.4 **Young People Survey**
Method of finding first job-employed sample

Method of finding job	First occupations								
	All	Management	Professional	Clerical	Other non-manual	Craft	Service and transport	Other manual	Other general labour
Base	1,778	23	101	459	175	476	149	290	105
	%	%	%	%	%	%	%	%	%
Newspaper	15	17	27	22	17	11	11	8	7
Personal contacts	15	13	12	10	14	15	19	19	24
Through family	16	13	10	12	11	18	20	23	20
Approached employer	15	13	8	11	18	17	16	18	14
Employer approached school/college	4	4	5	5	1	6	3	5	2
Jobcentre/ Employment Office	6	9	5	6	5	4	7	8	6
Careers Office	22	26	26	22	22	26	13	15	25
Private employment agency	3	—	2	9	1	*	—	*	—
Other	8	9	10	7	14	7	13	8	3
Don't know	1	—	1	1	1	*	—	1	1

(Percentages rounded; * less than 0.5).

Job-searching by young people

7.18 Young people in the surveys were asked how they had heard about their first job. Their answers, analysed by the type of job they entered, are shown in table 7.4.

7.19 In confirmation of the Employers Survey results, the Careers Office was the most important single method by which young people heard about their first jobs, and was particularly a source for non-manual, craft and general labourer jobs. Advertisements in newspapers were almost equally important for those entering non-manual jobs, while personal contacts, especially through the family, and contacting the employer directly were as important for those who entered manual jobs. For the bulk of those who entered semi- and unskilled manual jobs, including many of those now unemployed, personal contacts and recommendation by the family were the main methods through which they had heard about their jobs. Notably few young people had found jobs of any type through an employer's visit to school.

7.20 There were differences in the ways young people heard about their first job according to the level of qualifications they held. These differences are in fact related to those already mentioned since, as is shown in the next section, the type of job entered is related to the level of qualifications held. The well-qualified, those with 'A' level or 5 or more 'O' level GCEs, had most frequently heard about their job through newspapers: those with few qualifications, i.e. CSEs other than grade 1 or with no qualifications, were far more likely to have heard of their first job through personal contacts, through their families or by direct approach to employers.

7.21 Other surveys have found the Careers Service to be the most important single method by which young people find their first job (14). Studies have also noted that the least-qualified young person and those who left school at the earliest opportunity, giving reasons which indicate their dissatisfaction with school as did many young people in the Unemployed Survey, were less likely to use the Youth Employment Service (now called the Careers Service) than were other school-leavers (15). The explanation offered was that alienation from school, reflected in an eagerness to leave school as soon as possible, may extend to an alienation from 'officials' in general. Some young people may not use the official sources of help because they represent 'them' as opposed to 'us' and prefer to trust the informal job finding network of friends and relations or personal approaches to employers, which can supply them with jobs when the market is buoyant.

Conclusions

7.22 At a time when vacancies are scarce and young people are competing with many workers who are often more experienced, employers' criticisms of the attitudes and abilities of some young people coming to them for jobs, and their clear preferences for other workers, suggest some young job-seekers may experience serious difficulties. It seems that even if unemployment falls, employers may still prefer adults to young people – and while many adults are unemployed, young people will be at a disadvantage. Youth unemployment may, therefore, be a much longer-term problem. The new special programmes for unemployed young people aim to provide opportunities through which young people can develop their attitudes and abilities through work and training, thereby increasing their competitiveness.

7.23 While the 'official' job-placing agencies form an important part of the network by which employers fill non-manual and skilled manual jobs, their importance in filling other manual jobs is often equalled by the more informal network of recommendations by family and friends. These differences are reflected in the use young people make of the services: the better qualified making more use of the official agencies and the least qualified making more use of the more informal methods. This could be due, in part, to employers' failure to register many semi-skilled and unskilled jobs with the Careers Service and, in part, to the alienation from 'officials' of some young people.

Young people at work

Introduction

8.1 In this section we consider the experiences of young people at work: the jobs that they enter and those that they move to; the job mobility of young people; the reasons why young people change, or want to change, jobs; and the level of pay they receive.

First employment

8.2 Table 8.1 shows the first jobs of the employed and unemployed by sex, and table 8.2 shows first occupations by level of highest qualification. There are marked differences in both tables. Girls are more likely to enter clerical jobs; boys to enter craft jobs. About

Table 8.1

Nature of first job

| | Young People Survey (16 – 19) | | | | Unemployed Survey Survey (16 – 18) | | Training Survey | |
| | Employed | | Unemployed | | | | Employed and unemployed (16 – 24) | |
	Male	Female	Male	Female	Male	Female	Male	Female
Base	945	833	71	76	186	148	3,915	3,005
Occupations:								
Non-manual								
Management	2%	—	—	—	—	—	1%	1%
Professional	6%	6%	1%	1%	1%	2%	10%	9%
Clerical	9%	45%	6%	28%	2%	19%	11%	48%
Other non-manual	6%	14%	7%	11%	9%	17%	9%	14%
Manual								
Craft	41%	10%	24%	24%	19%	16%	34%	8%
Service and transport	6%	11%	10%	21%	6%	16%	12%	11%
Other manual	21%	11%	24%	12%	44%	28%	22%	9%
Other general labour	9%	3%	28%	4%	17%	1%	1%	—
Unclassified					3%	1%		

Industry of first employer

| | Young People Survey | | | | Unemployment Survey | |
| | Employed | | Unemployed | | | |
	Male	Female	Male	Female	Male	Female
Base	945	833	71	76	186	148
Industry						
Basic industries	7%	1%	3%	1%	5%	—
Manufacturing industries	34%	31%	31%	41%	40%	43%
Const. & build. industries	17%	2%	15%	1%	11%	1%
Gas, electricity and water	1%	1%	—	—	1%	—
Distribution, transport & communications	21%	24%	24%	26%	30%	39%
Insurance, banking and finance	4%	12%	—	1%	1%	5%
Professional & scientific services	2%	9%	1%	12%	2%	2%
Other services	11%	14%	21%	16%	7%	7%
Central and local govt.	4%	6%	4%	1%	3%	2%
Self employed/uncodable	1%	—	1%	—	1%	1%

one-third of both sexes are first employed in manufacturing industries, with distribution, transport and communications and the other services sector accounting for the next largest employment groups. This pattern of entry is similar to the last comprehensive statistical data of 1973 and has changed little over the last decade (16).

Table 8.2 **First job - highest qualification attained**

| | Young People Survey (16 – 19) | | | | | | | | | |
| | Employed | | | | | Unemployed | | | | |
	'A' levels and above	5 GCE 'O' or equiv.	1-4 GCE 'O' levels or equiv.	CSE not grade 1	No quali-fications	'A' levels and above	5 GCE 'O' levels or equiv.	1-4 GCE 'O' levels or equiv.	CSE not grade 1	No quali-fications
Base	139	186	454	553	446	8	2	26	28	83
Occupations:										
Non-manual										
Management	3%	4%	1%	1%	—	—	—	—	—	—
Professional	23%	16%	6%	2%	—	—	—	—	4%	1%
Clerical	41%	44%	35%	22%	9%	40%	—	31%	18%	11%
Other non-manual	7%	9%	11%	11%	9%	12%	—	12%	14%	6%
Manual										
Craft	12%	18%	28%	29%	31%	12%	—	23%	14%	29%
Service and transport	5%	5%	7%	10%	11%	12%	50%	15%	25%	12%
Other manual	8%	4%	10%	19%	28%	12%	—	19%	7%	22%
Other general labouring	1%	1%	3%	6%	12%	12%	50%	—	18%	19%

First job - highest qualification attained

| | Unemployed Survey (16 – 18) | | | | Training Survey (16 – 24) | | | | |
| | | | | | Employed and Unemployed | | | | |
	5 GCE 'O' levels or equiv.	1-4 GCE 'O' levels or equiv.	CSE not grade 1	No quali-fications	'A' levels and above	5 GCE 'O' levels or equiv.	1-4 GCE 'O' levels or equiv.	CSE not grade 1	No quali-fications
Base	9	49	94	182	980	530	1,246	1,324	2,835
Occupations:									
Non-manual									
Management	—	—	—	—	2%	2%	1%	1%	1%
Professional	—	6%	1%	—	39%	15%	8%	4%	2%
Clerical	22%	16%	14%	5%	29%	49%	43%	27%	15%
Other non-manual	—	2%	15%	11%	5%	9%	11%	9%	15%
Manual									
Craft	44%	14%	14%	19%	7%	12%	18%	34%	26%
Service and transport	—	8%	11%	12%	9%	5%	8%	11%	15%
Other manual	11%	33%	38%	38%	8%	8%	11%	14%	24%
Other general labouring	22%	4%	6%	13%	1%	—	—	—	2%
Unclassified	—	1%	—	2%					

Effect of qualifications on the type of job entered

8.3 There is a clear relationship between educational achievement and first job. Those with 'A' or 'O' level GCEs or equivalent were more likely to be in 'white-collar' jobs and those with CSEs less than grade 1 or no qualifications to be in 'blue-collar' jobs. The possession of qualifications was not shown to be a precondition of entry to skilled manual jobs – nearly a third of those who had entered craft jobs had no qualifications.

8.4 This is supported by the Employers Survey findings on the attributes employers said were essential and desirable in recruits to different levels of employment. For recruits of all ages, willingness and attitudes towards work were regarded as most essential attributes, followed by ability in the '3Rs'. Although employers did not generally attach great importance to specific educational qualifications, it seems probable that qualifications were regarded as an indication of the level of basic educational ability.

Table 8.3 — Present or most recent occupation

| | Young People Survey (16 – 19) | | | | Unemployed Survey (16 – 18) | | Training Survey (16 – 24) Employed | |
| | Employed | | Unemployed | | | | | |
	Male	Female	Male	Female	Male	Female	Male	Female
Base	945	833	71	76	186	148	3,549	2,803
Non-manual								
Management	2%	—	3%	—	—	—	3%	1%
Professional	6%	6%	1%	4%	1%	2%	13%	12%
Clerical	10%	45%	7%	21%	3%	20%	10%	48%
Other non-manual	5%	13%	10%	22%	7%	16%	6%	10%
Manual								
Craft	44%	10%	17%	12%	13%	11%	36%	7%
Service & transport	6%	10%	14%	16%	9%	20%	11%	11%
Other manual	21%	13%	21%	18%	47%	28%	20%	10%
Other general labour	7%	2%	27%	7%	17%	1%	1%	1%
					3%*	2%*		

*unclassifiable

Industry of present or most recent occupation

| | Young People Survey (16 – 19) | | | | Unemployed Survey (16 – 18) | |
| | Employed | | Unemployed | | | |
	Male	Female	Male	Female	Male	Female
Base	945	833	71	76	186	148
Basic industries	6%	1%	1%	4%	4%	—
Manufacturing industries	35%	32%	15%	28%	41%	43%
Const. & building industries	18%	2%	21%	4%	13%	1%
Gas, electricity and water	1%	1%	—	—	1%	1%
Dist., transport & commun.	20%	25%	31%	36%	28%	34%
Insurance, banking & finance	4%	11%	—	4%	1%	2%
Professional & scientific services	2%	9%	1%	9%	1%	2%
Other services	8%	12%	24%	12%	5%	12%
Central and local govt.	5%	8%	6%	4%	5%	2%
Self-emp. & uncodable	1%	—	1%	—	1%	2%

8.5 The required basic educational standards varied according to the type of job for which recruits were sought. Employers rated ability in the '3Rs' as essential for two-thirds of the non-manual jobs, a little over half the skilled manual jobs but only just over a fifth of the other manual jobs. Considerably more thought this attribute was either essential or desirable: 83% for non-manual jobs, 80% for skilled jobs but only 54% for other manual jobs. Lack of basic education was the second most important reason why employers rejected applicants to skilled manual and non-manual jobs, but was considerably less important as a reason for rejecting applicants for other manual jobs. Size and type of establishment also had a bearing on the emphasis placed on educational standards: larger firms and the more office-based industries being more likely to reject applicants on the grounds of their lack of basic education, lack of specific qualifications or poor performance in a test.

8.6 Employers said that willingness and attitudes to work were the most important attributes they looked for in recruits but qualifications, at least to a basic standard, are probably required of many recruits to skilled and non-manual jobs. Two other surveys sought information on employers' requirements for formal qualifications and reached similar conclusions. A survey of careers officers and employers (17) undertaken in 1972 showed that few employers had formal selection standards which favoured the qualified at the expense of the unqualified but that firms were more selective in times of high unemployment. Most firms emphasised, however, that personality, alertness and other personal qualities were more important than paper qualifications. A survey of employers in Leicestershire (18) confirmed that requirements for formal qualifications varied widely between work organisations except for unskilled jobs where general suitability or disposition were the most important factors.

Current employment

8.7 Table 8.3 shows current or most recent jobs by employment status and sex for the three young people surveys. The distribution overall differs little from that for first jobs, except that rather more of the unemployed had been in semi-skilled or unskilled manual jobs. The similarity in distribution is not surprising since two-thirds of the employed and 43% of the unemployed who had worked in the Young People Survey, and 45% of those in the Unemployed Survey who had worked, had had only one job. In the Training Survey 63% were still in their first type of work, although this does not necessarily mean the same job (see Technical Appendix).

8.8 The cross-classification of the details of occupation and industry for the employed young people in the Young People Survey showed a considerable concentration of employment, with 50% of the young people in only six industry/occupation areas:

craft occupations in manufacturing	14%
other manual occupations in manufacturing	10%
craft occupations in construction	7%
other non-manual occupations in distribution, transport and communications	7%
clerical occupations in insurance, finance and business services	6%
clerical occupations in distribution, transport and communications	6%

Occupational mobility

8.9 The Employers Survey shows the penetration by grade of young people (16–18 year olds) into the labour force. Young people accounted for 4% of employment across all grades although the penetration of young people was rather higher in skilled manual grades and non-manual grades, 9% and 6% respectively, but lower, 3%, in other manual grades. The latter is particularly significant since other manual grades accounted for the greatest proportion (46%) of total employees.

Place of young people in the labour force

8.10 Comparison of the first and current occupations and industries of those who had had more than one job shows that those who were employed had relatively high occupational stability while this was less true of the unemployed. The latter seemed to have suffered considerable 'downgrading' between their first and last jobs and had moved, in many instances, between the manufacturing and service sectors. The reasons for this included:—

a) involuntary termination of employment, owing to redundancy, dismissal or the end of short-term jobs, accounting for roughly one-third of cases;

b) voluntary termination, accounting, again, for roughly one-third of cases; and

c) a variety of causes, including medical reasons, some of which appeared to be attempts to disguise dismissal.

These suggest that many young people had been recruited during booms in the economy only to be dismissed or downgraded during the downturn in the cycle. They seem to support also the criticism of the motivation of some young people voiced by employers, though their low motivation could be due as much to their conditions of work as to their general attitude.

8.11 Evidence of 'downgrading' among job changers has been noted in other studies (19). These have shown the significance of distribution and some manufacturing as the first industries into which mobile people go; the likelihood that job changers will change industry and take up employment at a lower level; and that a higher proportion of frequent job changers fail to achieve their original vocational objectives.

Job mobility

8.12 Table 8.4 shows the number of jobs young people had had by their age and employment status. As would be expected the number of jobs increased with age. There was little difference between girls and boys in the number of jobs, but there were substantial differences between the employed and the unemployed – the latter being a much more mobile group. Those with few or no qualifications generally had had more jobs than the better qualified, though this could have been due, partly, to the former having left school earlier and so having been on the labour market for longer.

8.13 Young people are known to be more job mobile than their elders (20) and two explanations have been put forward for this (21). One is that the transition period and early years of employment are when young people decide on what jobs they want to do and so frequent job changing is regarded as 'job shopping.' The other holds that, rather than trying-out jobs, the young person, and especially the least able young person, is attempting to relieve the intrinsic boredom of the jobs he or she is able to get while maximising other benefits such as pay. Several questions in our survey threw some light

Table 8.4 **Number of jobs held** E=Employed 1,778 Respondents U=Unemployed 147 Respondents

No. of jobs held	16 years			17 years			18 years			19 years	
	Young People Survey		Unemployed Survey	Young People Survey		Unemployed Survey	Young People Survey		Unemployed Survey	Young People Survey	
Base	E	U	59	E	U	120	E	U	465	E	U
1	83%	72%	66%	72%	49%	54%	61%	33%	31%	54%	26%
2 – 5	17%	28%	34%	28%	49%	45%	38%	59%	65%	44%	71%
6 – 10	—	—	—	—	2%	1%	1%	8%	3%	2%	—
10+	—	—	—	—	—	—	—	—	—	—	3%

on these hypotheses by covering aspects such as the reasons why young people leave jobs, their satisfaction and dissatisfaction with jobs, whether they have thought of changing their job and whether they have changed their ideas about work.

Reasons for leaving jobs

8.14 66% of the employed in the Young People Survey were in their first jobs. For those that had had previous jobs the most common reasons for leaving their first job had been:

Base	594		%
	%	Movement to a better job	15
Insufficient pay	21	Dislike of the work	12
Boredom	15	Poor prospects	12

8.15 In 8.10 it is stated that many of the unemployed left their first job involuntarily: 44% of the unemployed in the Young People Survey and 53% of those interviewed for the Unemployed Survey had been either dismissed or made redundant from their last job, or had been in jobs which were short-term. The most important reasons for leaving voluntarily were dislike of the work and low pay. Typical replies were:

"I was doing nothing constructive."

"I left myself – I was getting fed up making tea and going out to get the dinners."

"I told him what to do with the job. I was told there would be a bonus and there wasn't."

"I was a junior – a girl left and I applied for her job. I got it, but I had to do my old job as well still for £12 per week."

Job satisfaction and dissatisfaction

8.16 The expectations young people have of jobs and the extent to which these expectations go unmet may explain high job-mobility among young people. A recent study of male school-leavers (22) found dissatisfaction in a job to be a good, though not the strongest, indication of a disposition to leave that job and to change jobs more frequently thereafter. To assess whether job dissatisfaction is a major factor in mobility the present surveys asked young people what they were looking for in a job and whether they were happy in their present or last job.

8.17 Table 8.5 shows the elements young people rated as important and as most important in a job. It is interesting that the unemployed and those who have experienced unemployment place pay rather higher than those who have been continually employed. One explanation for this, which other studies have also suggested (23), could be that many of the least able young people accept that they will have less interesting jobs and so focus their attention on compensating factors such as pay and conditions. It could also be that the financial hardship of unemployment has focused their attention on pay.

8.18 To some extent this is also confirmed by the answers given to questions about like or dislike of a job. The employed in the Young People Survey were asked: "Taking everything into account, would you say you are generally happy in your job?" The majority (89%) were generally happy and, when asked about any dislikes, 57% said there was nothing in particular they disliked about their job. This varied little according to the characteristics of the young people or according to the occupations and industries in which they were employed, except for those in other manual jobs and manufacturing industry where 16% in both cases expressed general unhappiness with their job (compared with 11% overall). The minority who did express dissatisfaction with aspects of their job gave a variety of reasons: the main ones were pay and, to a lesser extent, boring or uninteresting work with the latter being more important for those in other manual jobs or employed in manufacturing. The majority of young people (90%) also thought their 'boss' treated them fairly.

Table 8.5   **What things are important to you in a job?**

| | Young People Survey (16 – 19) | | | | Unemployed Survey (16 – 18) | |
| | Employed | | Unemployed | | | |
	and never been unemployed	and have been unemployed	and have worked	and have never worked	No work	Worked
Good money	494 44%	345 53%	74 50%	53 51%	129 60%	195 59%
Friendly atmosphere	638 57%	369 57%	72 49%	56 54%	89 42%	182 55%
Job satisfaction	477 43%	280 43%	44 30%	40 39%	20 9%	22 7%
Interesting work	155 14%	100 16%	21 14%	19 18%	74 35%	115 35%
Promotion opportunities	134 12%	68 11%	9 6%	11 11%	10 5%	31 9%
Good working conditions	301 27%	195 30%	38 26%	22 21%	28 13%	54 16%
Base	1,115 100%	645 100%	147 100%	103 100%	214 100%	329 100%

What is the most important thing in a job?

| | Young People Survey (16 – 19) | | | | Unemployed Survey (16 – 18) | |
| | Employed | | Unemployed | | | |
	and never been unemployed	and have been unemployed	and have worked	and have never worked	Never worked	Worked
Good money	106 10%	71 11%	22 15%	19 18%	45 21%	83 25%
Friendly atmosphere	207 19%	118 18%	29 20%	14 14%	36 17%	69 21%
Job satisfaction	458 41%	260 40%	36 24%	34 33%	10 5%	16 5%
Interesting work	55 5%	29 4%	5 3%	8 8%	46 22%	57 17%
Base	1,115 100%	645 100%	147 100%	103 100%	214 100%	329 100%

8.19 In the Unemployed Survey, young people were asked to grade their liking for their last job on a five-point scale ranging from 'liked it a lot' to 'did not like it at all', and to say which aspects of their job they had liked and disliked. Many more of these young people had been employed in the other manual category of jobs in manufacturing industry and consequently their answers can be regarded as a measure of the job satisfaction or dissatisfaction amongst those in semi- or unskilled manufacturing jobs where the work can often be dull and uninteresting. A high proportion (71%) said they had quite liked their job or liked it a lot although those who had had manual jobs had been rather less happy than those who had had non-manual jobs: 67% of the former quite liked their last job or liked it a lot, compared with 83% of the latter. Many seemed not to have strong feelings about their last jobs: 47% said there was nothing they had particularly disliked and 38% nothing they had particularly liked. The people worked with, specific aspects of the work and meeting people in the course of the work were aspects which had been liked most frequently. Specific aspects of the work and bad working conditions were most frequently disliked. As noted before, most young people (82%) had got on well with the people they worked for.

8.20 Young people seem generally to be satisfied with their jobs – even among those whose jobs might be least interesting. (However, it is recognised that people are generally reluctant to express dissatisfaction with their work.) For the most mobile group of young people (i.e. the unemployed and those who have experienced unemployment) pay and, to a lesser extent, good conditions and friendly people to work with were the elements looked for in a job. It seems that for many of these young people voluntary job changes are likely to be motivated by the desire to improve pay or conditions, perhaps as compensation for the less interesting nature of their jobs.

Changing jobs or ideas about work

8.21 Despite being generally happy in their job a third of the employed in the Young People Survey had thought seriously of changing their jobs. When probed as to the reasons why they had not done so, the most frequent answer (38% of all those who had thought of changing) was that there were no jobs available at the time. This suggests that the current state of the labour market is a constraint on the ambitions of many young people.

8.22 The Young People Survey asked if the young people's ideas about jobs had changed in the last two years and, if so, why. There was little difference between the proportions of employed and unemployed who had changed their ideas: 34% and 40% respectively. However, in both cases the better qualified were slightly more likely to have changed ideas than were the less qualified or unqualified. The main reasons for changing ideas were:

	employed	unemployed
base: all those who had changed ideas	610	99
	%	%
'Ideas change as you get older'	21	15
'The job I want has become more difficult to get'	15	25
'Jobs are generally scarce'	12	19

This supports the belief that the current state of the labour market is affecting occupational choice, especially for the unemployed.

Job mobility - conclusions

8.23 It seems that both hypotheses in 8.13 have some validity. Some young people do change jobs in an effort to find more interesting work and do use their early years of

Table 8.6   Comparison of the net pay of employed young people and unemployed young people (in most recent job)

Net pay	Employed (Young People Survey)				Unemployed (Unemployed Survey)		
	16	17	18	19	16	17	18
Up to £15	42 11.9%	39 8.9%	19 3.6%	12 2.9%	19 38%	31 28.7%	32 22.1%
£16 – £20	157 44.6%	131 29.5%	77 14.6%	31 7.4%	22 44%	52 48.1%	54 37.2%
£21 – £25	102 29%	169 38.1%	170 32.1%	78 18.7%	6 12%	19 17.6%	28 19.3%
£26 – £30	44 12.5%	72 16.2%	149 28.2%	111 26.6%	2 4%	3 2.8%	18 12.4%
£31 and over	7 2%	33 7.4%	114 21.6%	186 44.5%	1 2%	3 2.8%	13 9.0%
Base	352 100%	444 100%	529 100%	418 100%	50 100%	108 100%	145 100%

employment to formulate their ideas about jobs. For others, and especially the less able young person, movements are made involuntarily or to improve money and conditions, possibly as compensation for the less interesting nature of the work, while choice of job is largely determined by what is available on the local labour market.

Pay

8.24 Table 8.6 shows the net pay in the current job for the employed from the Young People Survey and for the last job of those in the Unemployed Survey. There are some marked differences in the levels of pay between the samples.

8.25 Those in the Unemployed Survey had received much lower levels of pay on average than the employed in the Young People Survey, although this can probably be explained by the much greater proportion of the unemployed who had been employed in unskilled manual jobs. Also many of the unemployed had been out of work for some time (just over half had been unemployed for six months or more), consequently their pay would relate to Phase I of pay policy, while the pay of the employed would relate to Phase II of pay policy.

Fair pay

8.26 Interviewees in the Young People Survey and the Unemployed Survey were asked what they thought was a fair take-home wage or salary for themselves: Table 8.7 shows the mean and median suggested levels of pay. In general, young people thought a fair level of pay to be a few pounds more than they were, or had been, earning.

8.27 In both surveys the most common reason given for mentioning a particular level of pay was that it was that which was needed to live on (29% in the Young People Survey and 33% in the Unemployed Survey). In the Unemployed Survey the next most important reasons were that it was about average or fair (16%) and that it was right for a person of the respondent's age (11%). In the Young People Survey the second most

Table 8.7

What do you think is a fair take-home wage/salary for you per week?

	Young People Survey		Unemployed Survey	
Age	Mean	Median	Mean	Median
	£	£	£	£
16	27.70	24.05	22.57	20.17
17	29.70	28.27	26.17	20.96
18	31.52	29.25	33.34*	31.09*
19	34.70	33.36	—	—

*Response to the Unemployed Survey included some young people who became 19 between initial contact being made and the interview being carried out.

important reason was that it was what the young person was, or had been, earning (26%). It is probable that the unemployed did not make reference as frequently to the pay they had experienced because their previous jobs generally had been less well paid.

Conclusions

8.28 The pattern of young people's employment has changed little over the last decade. About a third of young people are employed in manufacturing and substantial numbers are employed in distribution, transport and communications and the other services sector. Boys are more likely to enter craft jobs and girls to enter clerical jobs.

8.29 Despite a relatively high level of job-changing among young people most young people stay in the same occupation and industrial group. There is evidence, however, suggesting that those who change jobs most frequently are likely to suffer a down-grading in the type of job and to change industry. For the more frequent job changer, job changing seems to have either been involuntary or to have been motivated by a desire to improve money and conditions, possibly as compensation for the less interesting nature of their work. The availability of jobs on the local market often determines the jobs open to him or her and, it is not surprising that when jobs are generally scarce, such young people are likely to become unemployed. Although some changes of job can be beneficial, as they enable young people to widen their experience and, possibly, to increase their job satisfaction, the frequency with which some young people change jobs has a detrimental effect on their employment prospects.

8.30 From the levels of pay that young people said they were or had been earning, the unemployed were generally poorer paid in their last jobs, probably because many of them had been employed in semi- and unskilled manual jobs and because, for many, their pay relates to Phase I of pay policy. The level of pay regarded as fair by young people was not particularly high although in most cases it was slightly higher than they were receiving: in most cases it was felt that a young person needed that level of pay to live on.

Chapter 9

Training and further education

Introduction

9.1 Concern over training for young people has centred on two issues: the level of apprentice intake and fluctuations in that level caused by swings in the business cycle, and the large numbers of young people who leave school and enter work with little or no training. Little is known about the extent to which young people receive induction, training or further education after leaving school. To help fill this gap the surveys collected information on the numbers and characteristics of those young people receiving induction, training or further education; the types of training and further education received; and the attitudes of young people towards training.

Induction

9.2 64% of employers in the Employers Survey said they gave formal induction* to new recruits, although this varied according to the type of job: 76% of employers giving induction to recruits to skilled manual jobs, 62% to recruits to other manual jobs and 57% to recruits to non-manual jobs. Induction was more common in larger firms. There were no marked differences between industry groups except in the case of construction where only 22% of employers said they gave a formal induction to recruits.

9.3 36% of employers, mainly the larger firms, said they gave an induction programme which was specifically designed for young people. Skilled manual recruits were the most likely to receive such a programme (47%) and other manual recruits the least likely (23%). When asked to describe ways in which induction was geared specifically to young people, employers mentioned instruction on safety most frequently (16% of those giving induction specific to young people), followed by help in understanding processes in the factory or place of work (15%) and instruction in the differences between what was required of them by work and by school. Other features were health and medical advice; an introduction to the union; descriptions of the responsibilities of the job and to the firm; information about social activities; the history of the company; future prospects of the job; the standard of work required; and a 'dummy run' before starting the job itself.

9.4 These results are compatible with those of a recent study of the induction of school-leavers into work in Leicestershire (24), which found that all the work organisations involved structured the ways in which some information reached their new employees, although not always using formal induction programmes. The National Survey of Health and Development (NSHD) (25) also looked at induction and found that large firms were more likely than small ones to arrange satisfactory schemes of induction.

Receipt of training and further education

9.5 In recent years there has been concern over large numbers of young people who receive little or no planned training in their first job. As many as 300,000 a year have been estimated to come into this category (26). From the Young People Survey it is estimated that in 1974, 1975 and 1976 those young people receiving no planned training** in their first job were around 230,000, 200,000 and 260,000 respectively. (As the interviews took place in November 1976, the 1976 figure may be rather inflated).

9.6 Girls were less likely than boys to have received training in their first job: 45% of girls in the Training Survey received training in their first job compared with 58% of boys. Those with no qualifications or, to a lesser extent, high qualifications were also less likely to have received training in the first job: in the Training Survey only 46% of the unqualified and 51% of those with 'A' level GCEs or higher qualifications had received training compared with 59% of those with other qualifications.

---

*Employers were asked if they provided induction and training, and for some details about what type they provided. It was not generally possible to assess the quality and usefulness of the training or induction.

**The young people were asked whether they had received "any training or instruction in how to do the work (apart from any necessary introduction to people and procedures in the first few days of employment)." The findings indicate that young people generally made reference to more formal types of training and, in some cases, did not include forms of induction such as being shown how to do the job.

9.7 The unemployed in our surveys were less likely to have received training in their first job than were the employed. Only 26% of those in the Unemployed Survey who had worked and 41% of the unemployed in the Young People Survey who had worked had received training in their first job compared with 57% of those in the Young People Survey who were employed. These differences largely reflect variations between the employed and unemployed in level of educational ability and type of job entered.

9.8 It was noticeable that, among those in the Unemployed Survey who had worked, fewer of those who had left school at the earliest opportunity had received training in their first job (24%) than had those who had left school later (35%). A similar trend was found by the NSHD (27), which showed that for all young people those who had left school at the earliest opportunity were generally less likely to have received training than were later leavers.

9.9 On being asked whether they had ever received training or further education, nearly a third of 16-24 year olds questioned in the Training Survey said they had received no training and nearly two-thirds had received no further education. (The NSHD (28) found that 30% of young people in their 18th year were attending part-time further education). As before, girls and those with either no qualifications or higher qualifications were least likely to have received training. There was no appreciable regional difference.

Type of training and further education received

9.10 Tables 9.1 and 9.2 show information from the Employers Survey and from the Training Survey on the type of training young people received. While the format of the questions in the surveys was rather different the overall findings were broadly similar.

Table 9.1

Employers Survey - training
On-the-job training

	Grades			
	All grades	Skilled manual	Other manual	Non-manual
Base: all recruiting YPs	636	183	180	269
	%	%	%	%
Trained by supervisor	66	50	74	72
Trained by immediate work-mates	33	21	39	38
Formal apprentice training programme	27	68	7	12
Others	3	4	2	2
No real on-job training given	6	—	6	9

Off-the-job training

	All grades	Skilled manual	Other manual	Non-manual
Base: all recruiting YPs	636	183	180	269
	%	%	%	%
Day release	44	61	20	48
Evening classes	16	14	3	25
Establishment's own training centre	15	26	8	13
Full-time college for 1 year	7	21	2	—
Half-day release	5	4	2	—
Full-time college for 6 months	4	8	5	6
Full-time college for 2 or more years	1	3	—	—
Others	9	12	3	8
No off-job training given	34	7	69	28

Note: respondents sometimes did not distinguish between whole-day and half-day release, so the numbers may be somewhat biased towards whole-day release.

Table 9.2
Training Survey
Type of training received in first type of work and type of training ever received

No and % having never received training		Training in first type of work:	Type			Place		
No	%		basic	further	other	on-job	off-job	both
No	%	Training in first type of work: %	%	%	%	%	%	%
501	67	Managerial/professional	78	22	*	42	42	16
824	44	Clerical	75	23	2	44	51	5
242	31	Other non-manual	73	24	3	46	46	8
1321	85	Craft	91	9	*	47	36	17
301	38	Manual occupations in service and transport	88	12	1	61	30	9
466	42	Other manual	91	9	*	56	32	13
3	5	General labouring	33	67	—	50	50	—
4867	69	Training ever received	78	21	1	49	38	14

*Less than 0.5%.
N.B. %s for types of training received relate to training occasions, not to numbers of people having received training. It was possible for a person to have had more than one training occasion.

9.11 Systematic training was much more common for skilled manual jobs than for other categories; this took the form of programmes of apprenticeship combined with off-the-job training, either through day or block release. The few apprenticeships in other manual grades were mainly in processing or service industries such as catering and hairdressing, while those in non-manual occupations were mainly for technicians or professional trainees.

9.12 Young people employed in other manual grades had seldom received off-the-job training. The pattern of provision of further education for young people in employment seems to have changed little since the late 1960s when a survey of boy school-leavers (29) showed that apprentices were most likely to receive further education, followed by those in 'white-collar' jobs, while those in manual non-apprentice jobs were much less likely to have received any form of training.

9.13 The Employers Survey shows that formal apprenticeships were most common in the fabrication industries (42%) and far less common in the textile industry, where 84% of training was done mainly by supervisors. In general, young people recruited in small establishments were less likely to have undertaken a formal apprenticeship and more likely to have received no training. Other studies have also noted a relationship between the size of firm and the quality or 'intensity' of training, with large firms generally providing the best training (30).

9.14 Young people reported that most of the training received was to teach them the basic skills of the job rather than to upgrade these skills or retrain them for other tasks.

Table 9.2 (cont)

Timing		Paid for by		Duration				
full-time	part-time	employer	other	up to 4 weeks	4 weeks – 26 weeks	26 weeks – 1 year	1 year – 3 years	3 years or more
%	%	%	%	%	%	%	%	%
73	27	61	39	21	20	20	30	9
72	28	58	42	52	27	11	9	1
69	31	58	42	50	21	15	12	2
84	16	65	35	13	19	17	27	25
81	19	55	45	27	20	15	33	5
81	19	54	46	29	24	17	17	13
100	—	100	—	100	—	—	—	—
76	24	59	41	33	24	14	19	10

Training, generally, was full time, on-the-job and paid for by their employer. It either lasted a short while, usually a few weeks, or was considerably longer as in the case of apprenticeships where training often lasts three to four years.

Other help and assistance in learning the job

9.15 Most young people received some help and assistance in learning their job, usually as the Employers Survey shows, from supervisors and workmates. In the Training Survey, young people were asked about a variety of activities which they might have undertaken to help them learn their job but which they might not have thought of as 'training.' Their answers, shown in table 9.3, confirm that the most common activities were watching others and being taught or helped: these were followed by being sent round departments, reading, and practice in making things. Those employed in the other non-manual category of occupations e.g. shop assistants, or in manual occupations in service and transport industries were least likely to have undertaken these activities: these activities were most common among those in professional and craft occupations, who also received considerable formal training.

Attitudes towards training and further education

9.16 The interviewees in the Training Survey were asked whether they had tried and failed to get a specific training; whether they had ever turned down an offer of training; and whether they had ever been willing to undertake training.

9.17 Very few young people had tried and failed to get a specific training (9% of young men and 5% of young women) or had been offered training but turned it down (8% of young men and 5% of young women). However, a large number (80% of young men and 74% of young women) said they would be willing to undertake training if offered the chance.

Table 9.3 **Training Survey**
First type of work by other training activities (16-24 year olds)

	Total	Make things for practice	Special talk or lectures	Watched others	Sent round de-partments	Read things	Taught or helped	Refresher courses	None of these
Non-manual									
Management	69	28%	26%	81%	43%	51%	84%	7%	4%
Professional	676	40%	24%	78%	50%	72%	82%	10%	3%
Clerical	1,875	18%	13%	71%	67%	35%	82%	5%	3%
Other non-manual	776	15%	20%	71%	76%	28%	76%	5%	2%
Manual									
Craft	1,558	49%	20%	88%	59%	43%	87%	7%	4%
Service and transport	786	25%	14%	65%	77%	23%	68%	5%	3%
Other manual	1,114	26%	14%	79%	69%	24%	81%	3%	2%
Other general labouring	57	19%	2%	51%	82%	14%	37%	—	5%

9.18 45% were willing to train for their present job while a quarter expressed their willingness to train for a different job. The main benefits of such training were seen as increased earnings (83%), help in finding better jobs (78%), and greater job interest (77%) and satisfaction (76%).

9.19 Those who had no qualifications and those who had left school at 15 showed rather less enthusiasm for training; 29% and 28% respectively were not willing to train as opposed to 22% overall. There were also slight regional differences; those in Greater London were more willing to train (86%) and those in Wales and Scotland rather less willing (72% and 74% respectively).

Conclusions

9.20 The surveys confirmed that many young people do not receive formal training or further education. As many as a third of the 16-24 year olds said they had received no formal training and two-thirds said they had received no further education. Young women were particularly likely to have received no training.

9.21 The data shows that the pattern of provision of training has changed little over the years. Craft jobs stand out as being most likely to provide systematic training, usually in the form of an apprenticeship combined with day or block release. Larger firms generally provide more intensive training and are more likely to provide any training.

9.22 The surveys suggest a majority of young people would be willing to undertake training; nearly half preferring to undertake training for their present job but a quarter wanting to train for a different job. Training was seen as helping them increase their earnings, find a better job or make their job more interesting and satisfying. Overall, these findings indicate a demand for greater training provision, both to help young people improve their performance in jobs and to help them achieve their occupational ambitions.

PART III

Appendix and details

THE SURVEYS

Young people survey **1.1** The survey results are based on analysis of interviews with a total of 3,074 young people, aged 16–19 years, spread throughout Great Britain.

1.2 The sample design was a multi-stage stratified random sample, involving selection, initially, of parliamentary constituencies then polling districts and, within polling districts, clusters of addresses. A total of approximately 36,000 addresses was drawn and these formed the initial screening sample that interviewers were to contact in order to establish whether or not the household contained any 16–19 year olds. Where the presence of a 16–19 year old was identified the interviewer had to attempt to achieve an interview with that young person, a minimum of four recalls being necessary before the young person was classified as 'not available'. Fieldwork took place between 20 November 1976 and 4 December 1976 after piloting of the questionnaire over the previous month.

1.3 The screening sample identified 4,089 16–19 year olds and interviews were carried out with 3,099 (25 completed interviews arrived too late for processing and this reduced the number of interviews analysed to 3,074).

1.4 Of the 990 young people not interviewed 25% were excluded from the sample on the grounds that they were undertaking a full time degree or teacher training course, 28% proved impossible to contact and a further 22% refused to be interviewed. The remaining 25% were not interviewed for a variety of less individually significant reasons. The response rate of those eligible for interview was 81%.

1.5 An attempt was made to establish the sex and colour of non-respondents not in higher education in order to examine whether, on these two aspects, they were unrepresentative of the main sample. It was not always possible to obtain such information because in some cases interviewers were refused by parents, in others they had only been told by neighbours that young people were resident at the address and in others the interviewers did not complete the information. However, for those cases where information was obtained, males were disproportionately represented compared with the total sample (they accounted for 57% of non-respondents but only 50% of the total sample). There was no difference with respect to colour.

Unemployed survey **2.1** The survey interviewed 549 16–18 year olds registered with ten Unemployment Benefit Offices at the beginning of December 1976. The offices chosen, and the numbers ultimately interviewed who were registered at each, are shown in the table below:

Unemployment Benefit Office	Number interviewed
London – Camden Town	19
– Bexley	17
Glasgow – Parkhead	121
Liverpool – Walton	176
Smethwick	36
Huddersfield	44
Blyth	25
Worcester	42
St. Austell	32
Abertillery	37

The choice of offices was made so as to give a spread of areas broadly representative of the different types of area in the country as a whole.

2.2 Cards explaining the reasons for the survey and inviting co-operation were handed to all those aged 16–18 registered at these offices. Those willing to co-operate filled in their names and addresses on the cards and returned them. Approximately 40% of those registered did so and from these, names and addresses were selected by a random sampling method, after discarding those that were incomplete or unreadable, so that the final issued sample of 650 names and addresses was representative of the sex and age distributions of each register and of the sizes of the different Benefit Office registers.

2.3 Fieldwork took place between 13 January and 7 February 1977, after piloting of the questionnaire during December 1976 and a success rate of 85% was achieved, 553 interviews being carried out. Two questionnaires became unusable due to damage in the post and a further two were rejected as incomplete during editing. The total number of questionnaires analysed was, therefore, 549.

2.4 The Unemployed Survey was not based on a strictly random sample of unemployed 16–18 year olds (largely because the generation of such a sample would have been prohibitively expensive and time consuming) and this, combined with the voluntary nature of participation in the survey, could have lead to bias in the sample. Comparison of the characteristics of the Unemployed Survey sample with data from the other surveys, and from other sources, suggests the sample is somewhat biased in two ways. First, the Unemployed Survey contains a larger proportion of unemployed 16–18 year olds in conurbations than was found in the 1975 National Training Survey:

	Conurbation	Urban	Rural
	%	%	%
1975 National Training Survey	30	50	20
1977 Unemployed Survey	61	27	12

Second, the Unemployed Survey contains more long term unemployed than were interviewed in the Young People Survey or were recorded in the January 1977 Department of Employment unemployment statistics (see Table 3.1). Whenever this bias has been thought to affect the findings an indication has been made in the text.

Employers survey

3.1 The questionnaire for the Employers Survey was composed of two parts: an initial 'screening' section, carried out normally (other than in the case of shops) by telephone; and an extended follow-up section carried out mainly by personal interview.

3.2 In the screening phase of the survey 1,137 employers were contacted and simple information regarding employee numbers and occupations was recorded. Respondents were asked whether they had recruited any 16–18 year olds during 1976. 68% of the screening sample had done so and extended interviews were sought with these employers. The main part of the study then took the form of a series of extended interviews carried out with 701 employers of the 775 employers screened as eligible in the first stage. These were supplemented by interviews at head offices of 18 major enterprises and public corporations.

3.3 Interviewing was carried out between 10 November and 10 December 1976 and respondents were the personnel manager or senior person responsible for young people recruitment policies within the establishment. Interviewing was carried out throughout Great Britain in a total of 65 individual interviewing locations. The results were weighed to be representative of the 'universe' covered, which corresponds to factories with 50 or more employees, shops with 5 or more employees, construction firms with 25 or more employees, other establishments with 25 or more employees and all local authorities.

3.4 Details of the sample methods were as follows, establishments being identified from four separate sources:

General employers sample

This was selected from the IFF 'Master File' of key non-domestic establishments in Great Britain. This covers establishments of all types – factories, offices, warehouses, utilities, consumer services, etc. (Shops, construction firms and local authorities were excluded from the File and sampled separately, see below). Establishments were selected with probability proportional to size to ensure adequate coverage of larger employers. 783 establishments were drawn from the Master File and contacted in the screening stage. Of these, 524 had recruited at least one 16–18 year old during 1976, and were interviewed in full.

Shops

Shops with 5 or more employees were sampled by means of a 'random walk' technique. In total 241 such shops were located and screened, and full interviews carried out with 93 of them.

Construction firms

Construction firms with 25 or more employees were sampled from a separate file developed by IFF. A total of 64 was screened and 39 full interviews carried out with firms who had recruited a young person in 1976.

Local authorities

Contact was made with the person responsible for central recruitment in 49 local authorities across the country. Full interviews were held with 45 of these.

3.5 Results for the total of 1,137 establishments included in the screening stage as described above were weighted as shown in the table below:

Sector	Estimated total employment		Unweighted sample distribution	Weighted sample distribution	Basis of weighting
	Number	%			
General employers sample	13.46m	82.5	783	935	IFF estimates based on "Master File"
Shops with more than 5 employees	1.03m	6.3	241	72	Census of Distribution (1971)
Construction firms with more than 25 employees	0.85m	5.2	64	59	Private Contractors Census (1974)
Local Authorities	0.98m	6.0	49	68	Department of Employment – local authority employment classified to SIC 906
	16.32m	100	1,137	1,134*	

*The difference between the unweighted and weighted totals arises from the technique of weighting.

Training survey

4.1 The Training Survey was a special analysis carried out on data already collected for the National Training Survey, which had been undertaken in 1975 for the Training Services Agency.

4.2 The National Training Survey involved personal interviews with individuals in the age groups 16–64 for males and 16–69 for females and was based on a two-stage, stratified random sample. Both those living in private households and in institutions were included while current members of the Armed Forces were in general excluded.

4.3 The sampling frame included all local authority areas in Great Britain (excluding Northern Ireland and the more outlying Scottish Islands) and using systematic random sampling the first stage identified 2,575 polling districts within local authority areas which had been stratified successively according to:—

(i) The Registrar General's Planning Regions

(ii) their character as conurbation, urban or rural

(iii) a measure of population density or level of employment

(iv) a socio-economic index based upon the proportion of the population falling within the Registrar General's 'Professional and Managerial' occupation groups.

4.4 The second stage identified the resident population aged 16 and over within the two categories of elector and non-elector using systematic random sampling procedures. The total response rate was approximately 74% and data for just over 54,000 individuals, representing approximately 2 in 1,000 of the civilian working population, was obtained for analysis.

4.5 The preliminary pilot and technical studies stage of the National Training Survey was completed in the spring of 1975 and was followed by the main stage of the survey conducted over the period May 1975 to March 1976.

4.6 From the entire data set of the survey, the results of which are currently under analysis and are to be published in the near future, an 'extraction tape' of 16–24 year olds was prepared. The data for this group, which covered approximately 4,000 males and 3,000 females, formed the basis for the special analysis of young people carried out for the Working Party.

In view of the fact that the inclusion, in their entirety, of the questionnaires used in the surveys would have added considerably to the bulk of this publication, it was felt better to indicate the areas of questioning in the following tables.

Interested parties are invited to contact MSC if they wish to see the full versions of the questionnaires employed.

Young people survey The questionnaire for this survey was composed of four sections – the education and training section, the employed section, the unemployed section and the general section. Each respondent answered one of the first three sections, according to their status, and the general section.

Area of questioning	Details	Asked of
Current experience	Type of institution attended; who pays fees/costs; exams aimed for; reasons for doing course; length of time expect to continue; reasons for starting studying after being employed or unemployed; perceived ease of getting a job on leaving.	Those in further education/training
Current employment experience	Occupation; industry; length of time in job; how first heard about job; why they think they got the job; training received (length, full or part-time); happiness in job; treatment by employers; thoughts about changing job.	Employed
Past employment experience	First job – occupation; industry; length of time in job; training; how heard about job; reasons for leaving.	All
	Last job – occupation; industry; length of time in job; how heard about; why they think they got the job; training. Number of jobs held; reason for leaving last job.	Unemployed
		Employed and unemployed
	Total length of time in employment.	Those in FE/training
Current unemployment experience	Length of time unemployed; whether registered for employment, and reasons why not; methods of job search; number of jobs applied to; reasons why did not get last job applied to; number of times offered a job and turned it down, and reasons why.	Unemployed
Past unemployment experience	Number of times unemployed; longest period unemployed.	Employed and unemployed
	Total length of time unemployed.	All
Experience of work whilst at school	Holiday/spare time job; work experience arranged by school; community or voluntary work undertaken whilst at school; usefulness of such experiences.	All
Attitudes to work	Things important in a job; most important thing in a job; wage or salary per week thought fair and why; whether have changed mind in the last two years about the type of job job wanted, and why.	All

Area of questioning	Details	Asked of
Attitudes towards help for young people	Whether there is enough help for unemployed young people and, if not, who could do more and how; willingness to move to get a job.	Unemployed
	Whether seriously thought of going back to school or on to college and, if so, why not done so; willingness to take the chance to go back to school or on to college now and, if not, why.	Employed and unemployed
	Rated importance of elements of present and potential government schemes; fair pay from government for temporary work or training; willingness to do community work.	All
Classification and personal details	Age, sex, social class, marital status, residency, age left school, year left school, country of origin, qualifications, net income per week, presence of parents at interview.	All

Unemployed survey

Area of questioning	Details
Full-time education	Details of last school attended; time spent there; numbers of schools attended and reasons for attending more than 2; prolonged absence from school owing to illness; attitudes to school; truancy; examinations entered/passed; vocational advice from careers teachers, other teachers, careers officers or parents, whilst at school; age of leaving school and reasons for leaving, advice about leaving school; full-time FE/training undertaken immediately after leaving school, and reasons for doing so; type of institution; type and length of course; qualifications obtained; vocational advice received there.
	Ideas about type of work wanted on leaving full-time education, and reasons for this; job search before leaving full-time education.
Further education	Full/part-time courses taken since leaving full-time education; institutions attended; nature of the course; qualifications obtained; perceived value of the course.
Experience of work whilst at school	Holiday/spare time job, work experience arranged by school/college, voluntary work; evaluation of usefulness of experience.
Employment experience	Employment history since leaving school: length of time worked, length of time unemployed; number of jobs since school/college; job details (recorded for up to 3 jobs): length of time spent in job, method of finding job, selection for job, perceived reason for being given job, occupation, industry, training in job, attitudes to job, relationships with colleagues and supervisors, pay and promotion prospects, reason for leaving job, whether another job arranged before leaving.
Unemployment	Whether unemployed immediately after leaving school; methods of job search during this period; number of jobs applied for before obtaining first job.
	Experience during present or most recent period of unemployment: expectations about finding a job, methods of job search at beginning and end of period, reasons for any changes in job search, number of jobs applied for, type of job applied for at beginning

Area of questioning	Details
Unemployment (cont)	and end of period; reason for any change; any job offers refused and reasons for refusing; source and amount of income during unemployment; other activities during unemployment.
	Current job preferences and reasons for choice; expectations of obtaining this type of work; expectations of obtaining any job. Any opportunities to take classes/training courses whilst unemployed, but not taken, and reasons for not doing so. Attitudes of parents/friends to their unemployment; number of friends currently unemployed.
Agencies used in job search	Frequency of visits to careers offices, Jobcentres and private agencies by those unemployed immediately after leaving school/college; value of help/advice given. Frequency of visits to above agencies during present or most recent period of unemployment; value of help/advice given; changes in the frequency of such visits and reasons for change.
Attitudes to work	Things important in a job; most important aspect of a job; Assessment of fair weekly pay; reasons for thinking it fair.
Attitudes to help for young people	Is enough being done to help young people, what else could be done and by whom. Attitudes towards moving home to obtain a job, returning to school or going on to college, or taking a training they wanted to do. Evaluation of features from current and potential schemes; assessment of fair weekly wage for temporary work and for training; willingness to do community work.
Background and classification details	Sex, age, marital status, number of children, birthplace, members in the household, relationships of others in household and their occupational status, type of accommodation, length of time since living with father/mother, if not doing so, parents' occupation, length of any current parental unemployment.

National training survey

Area of questioning	Details
Full-time education	Type of school/college last attended full-time. Age of leaving, qualifications obtained.
Adult/further education	Courses taken after leaving full-time education, details of the 3 most recent types of institution, full/part-time or sandwich course, date and length of course, qualifications obtained.
Employment experience	Employment history since leaving school – duration of all changes in economic status – unemployment (periods of less than 3 months not recorded); employment. Details of all major changes of employer involved; whether moving home involved; description of main tasks in occupation, whether work was full or part time; numbers of employers worked for in each type of occupation; duration of employment with each employer; reasons for stopping that type of work; size of present firm (number of employees); number of other jobs held, and description of main other job; industry of main other job and total hours worked (for current work period only).

Area of questioning	Details
Training	Training received in/for each different occupation; purpose of training; what it involved; location; on/off-the-job; whether during working hours; who paid fees; type of firm worked for; length and date of training; full/part time; qualifications needed as prerequisite; whether course completed; if not, why not; qualifications obtained; what course led to; any other activities undertaken in first and present occupations which helped in learning the job. Whether tried at any time to obtain training, but not succeeded; last occasion tried, occupation at the time, occupation training was for, what training would have involved, length of course, who would have paid, reasons for not obtaining training. Ever turned down offer of training, last occasion this happened, occupation engaged in, occupation training was for, length of course, who would have paid, what course would have involved, reasons for turning it down. Any circumstances under which would now undertake training, would it be for present or different occupation, what value would the training have.
Classification/personal details	Age, sex, marital status, age and employment status of members of household, country of origin, country of origin of parents, year of entry to UK, membership of unions/associations, gross earnings, region (i.e. UK standard statistical region of current residence).

Employers survey

Area of questioning	Details
Organisation of the work force within the firm	Total numbers employed in 1971 and 1976; total numbers and numbers of 16 – 18 year olds employed in each grade in 1976; jobs likely to increase or decrease in importance in the next five years, and whether these jobs are likely to become more or less suitable for 16–18 year olds; likely changes in importance of 16–18 year olds within the firm in the next 5 years.
Recruitment practices in general	Is policy on recruitment governed by head office (if any); is recruiting done centrally or is there departmental responsibility; methods of recruiting; parts of the labour market which recruits are drawn from; formal practices governing recruitment; essential and desirable characteristics in recruits; numbers recruited by grade in previous 12 months; jobs for which it is difficult to get suitable recruits; affect on recruitment of an increase or decrease in business over the next 12 months.
Recruitment practices with respect to 16-18 year olds	Reasons for not recruiting any 16–18 year olds (ever or in last 5 years); method of deciding how many 16–18 year olds to recruit each year for each grade; numbers recruited in previous 12 months; expected recruitment in 1976; jobs for which it is difficult to attract 16–18 year olds; changes in the calibre of 16–18 year olds applying for jobs in the last 5 years; essential and desirable characteristics – how young people compared with older workers; reasons for rejecting 16–18 year olds; influence that increased availability of young people has had on recruitment; methods of recruitment and selection of applicants; opinion of how well briefed 16–18 year olds are about the job, the firm and how to behave at the interview, and whose responsibility it is to inform them, has age at which 16–18 year olds received the adult wage affected recruitment.
Induction and training	Is formal induction given to all workers, and to 16–18 year olds; how is induction geared to 16–18 year olds; what on and off job training is given to 16–18 year olds.

Area of questioning	Details
Knowledge and attitude towards government measures to help the unemployed	Knowledge of TES, RSSL, JCP, WEP, ITB special measures; use made of them; measures considered but not used, and why not; any scheme or circumstances (except an upturn in business) which would encourage recruitment of 16–18 year olds.
Details of firm and respondent	Type of establishment; main business activity of the company; total numbers employed by parent organisation (if any); length of time respondent has worked for firm; age of respondent.

Characteristics of the samples achieved for the Young People Survey and the Unemployed Survey

1.1 The following paragraphs show the samples achieved by the Young People Survey and by the Unemployed Survey with respect to sex, age, social class and educational qualifications, where possible compared with national statistics.

Sex and age profiles of the samples

1.2 The tables below display the sex and age breakdown of the Young People Survey sample compared with a similar population breakdown based on the Mid-Year Estimates of Population published in the *Annual Abstract of Statistics*.

Young People Survey 1976				Mid-year population estimates 1976*			
	Males	Females	All		Males	Females	All
16	16.2%	16%	32%	16	13.1%	12.4%	25.6%
17	13.4%	14.6%	28%	17	13%	12.3%	25.3%
18	12%	11.3%	23%	18	12.8%	12.1%	25%
19	8.8%	7.7%	16.5%	19	12.4%	11.8%	24.2%
	50.4%	49.6%	100%		51.3%	48.7%	100%

*Source: *Annual Abstract of Statistics*.

1.3 As will be seen the sample achieved was well representative with respect to the sex breakdown but not so with respect to age. The under-representation of 19 year olds is a reflection of the fact that full-time students in higher education or teacher training colleges were excluded from the sample, while the over-representation of 16 year olds, and to a lesser extent 17 year olds, probably reflects the greater ease with which the youngest people in the age group can be contacted at home.

1.4 The tables below display the sex and age breakdown of the Unemployed Survey sample compared with figures derived from the Mid Year Population Estimates. Since the Unemployed Survey did not seek to contact 19 year olds the comparative data is presented for 16, 17 and 18 year olds only.

Unemployed Survey 1977				Mid-year population estimates 1976			
	Males	Females	All		Males	Females	All
16	15%	15%	30%	16	17%	16%	34%
17	19%	16%	36%	17	17%	16%	33%
18	15%	15%	30%	18	17%	16%	33%
19	3%	1%	4%		—	—	—
	53%	47%	100%		51%	48%	100%

1.5 As will be seen the sample did in fact include a small number of 19 year olds who reached their 19th birthday during the period between initial contact being made and the young person being interviewed. Taking this factor into account it seems that the sample contacted had a similar sex and age structure to the population, indicating that the impact of unemployment is not age or sex biased.

Social class profiles of the samples

1.6 The table below shows the social class profile of the Young People Survey sample compared with national figures for the same categories:

Social class of parent	Young People Survey				National comparative figures*
	All	Education sub-sample	Employed sub-sample	Unemployed sub-sample	
	3,075	997	1,778	250	20,000
	%	%	%	%	%
AB	18	36	10	4	15.59
C1	19	22	18	12	21.47
C2	39	28	45	38	35.16
DE	23	13	25	42	27.77
	100	100	100	100	100

*Supplied by NOP Market Research Limited.

1.7 The Young People Survey employed the standard market research social grading (described below) and it will be seen that the representation achieved by the sample was good overall. More interesting are the pronounced differences between the three sub-samples: the A, B and C1 categories comprise 37% of the sample but only 16% of the unemployed and as much as 58% of those in education. However, grading of social class was based on the respondent's statement of parent's occupation and might accordingly be prone to some error.

1.8 The table below shows the definitions of social class, as used by the Institute of Practitioners in Advertising, and used by NOP Market Research Ltd. for the Young People Survey:

	Social class	Occupation of head of household
A	Upper Middle Class	Higher managerial, administrative or professional.
B	Middle Class	Intermediate managerial, administrative or professional.
C1	Lower Middle Class	Supervisory or clerical and junior managerial, administrative or professional.
C2	Skilled Working Class	Skilled manual workers.
D	Working Class	Semi- and unskilled manual workers.
E	Those at the lowest levels of subsistence	State pensioners etc., with no other earner.

1.9 The table opposite shows a similar comparison for the data of the Unemployed Survey. The coding of social class in this survey was based on the Census socio-economic groups and comparative data from the General Household Survey is presented.

1.10 It will be seen that respondents to the Unemployed Survey were significantly less likely to come from households in the first two socio-economic groups, but this is not surprising in view of the under-representation of A, B, and C1 groups found in the Unemployed sub-sample of the Young People Survey. The rather large number of unclassified responses in the Unemployed Survey may be a reflection of the fact that the parents of a substantial number of the respondents were themselves unemployed.

Socio-economic group	Unemployed Survey Parent's occupation	General Household Survey 1973 Head of household occupation
	%	%
Professional/employer/manager	3	17
Intermediate and junior non-manual	6	19
Skilled manual	47	33
Semi-skilled manual	20	19
Unskilled manual	10	6
Forces, unclassifiable, not stated	13	6
Base	549	11,342

Educational qualifications

1.11 The table below shows the samples achieved by the Young People Survey and the Unemployed Survey split by highest level of qualification obtained.

Highest educational level obtained	Young People Survey (16 – 19 year olds)			Unemployed Survey (16 – 18 year olds)
	Education sub-sample	Employed sub-sample	Unemployed sub-sample	
	977	1,778	250	549
	%	%	%	%
'A' Level GCE's or equivalent	8	8	8	—
5 or more 'O' Level GCE's or equivalent	37	10	4	4
1 – 4 'O' Level GCE's or equivalent	20	26	17	15
CSE's other than grade 1/ other qualifications	10	31	22	28
No qualifications	25	25	48	53

1.12 There are striking differences between the sub-samples and the surveys. Those still in full-time education are best qualified, while the employed are slightly less qualified and the unemployed very much less qualified. In both surveys about half the unemployed had no qualifications.

Coding of occupations

1.1 The occupations discussed in the Employers Survey were coded simply as follows:

Skilled Manual – any job requiring two or more years of training

Other Manual   – semi- or unskilled manual jobs

Non-manual   – general office activities plus retail and selling jobs. A very limited number of 'technician' jobs were discussed in detail under this heading.

1.2 The occupational codings employed for the Young People Survey, the Unemployed Survey and for the Training Survey were the same. These were based on a condensed form of the Department of Employment's list of key occupations for statistical purposes (KOS) major groups (31). This was modified along the lines of the classification used by the Department of Employment to show unemployment and vacancy statistics, the main change being a split of manual occupations between craft and non-craft. Table 1 shows the classification used for the surveys and Table 2 a reconciliation with KOS major groups.

1.3 The coding of occupations for the young people surveys was based on questions of the form:

"What type of work do you do? (probe as appropriate). Does the work have a name or a title? Is it manual or non-manual? What do you yourself make or do? What do you do most of the time? In what section/department do you work? What sort of machine/materials do you use?"

In the Young People Survey and the Unemployed Survey the question was asked in relation to a job, i.e. a period of time spent with one employer. In the Training Survey the question related to the whole period spent in an occupation, which could have been served with several employers.

Coding of industries

1.4 The industries in which respondents to the Young People Survey and the Unemployed Survey worked or had worked were coded according to a condensed version of the 1968 Standard Industrial Classification orders, while the respondents to the Employers Survey were coded according to a slightly different condensed version. The groups used for coding are shown in Table 3.

1.5 In the case of the young people surveys the coding was based on questions of the form:

"What is the main type of activity of your employer at the place where you worked or work for? (Probe). What does your employer do/make at the place where you work from? What is your employer's name?".

Table 1   **Occupational classification employed in the young people surveys**

Non-manual

a) Managerial — Main function is the planning, organisation, co-ordination or control of work and resources usually through other managers or supervisors, e.g. manager (or trainee) in works, production, stores, offices, shops, or farms. (Excluding supervisors.)

b) Professional and Related — e.g. Advertising executive; articled clerk; buyer; commercial artists; computer programmer; estate agent; estimator; information officers; insurance assessor; insurance broker; journalist; laboratory technician/assistant; market research analyst; medical technician; nurse; personnel officer; professional engineer/scientist; social worker; teacher; technician; therapist; window dresser; work study officer; engineering technician. (Excludes nursery nurse and dental technician.)

c) Clerical and Related e.g. Book-keeper; cashier; check-out operator; clerk specialising in wages; invoices, insurance, despatch, sales, freight, filing; data processing equipment operators; pay-out clerk; postman; receptionist; secretary; telephonist; typist. (Includes supervisors of above)

d) Other Non-manual including selling and security e.g. Commercial traveller; commodity broker; demonstrator; door-to-door canvassers; fireman; insurance agent; park-keeper; petrol pump/forecourt attendant; policeman/woman; roundsman; sales representative; sales staff; security guard; shop assistant; traffic warden.

Manual
e) Craft and Similar e.g. Baker; bricklayer; butcher; carpenter; clothing cutter; compositor; decorator; dental technician; dressmaker; electrician; electro typer; engineering craftsman; gas fitter; joiner; knitter; motor vehicle mechanic (skilled); painter; plumber; printing machine minder; radio/TV mechanic; sewing machinist; sheet metal worker; tailor; weaver; welder (skilled); woodworking machinist.

f) Manual Occupations in Service or Transport e.g. Caretaker; cleaner; cloakroom attendant; cook; counter hand (cafe or restaurant); hairdresser; hall porter; kitchen hand; laundry worker; maid; night porter; nursery nurse; porter; road sweeper; school helper; ticket collector; waiter; ward orderly.

g) Other Manual Occupations including Farming and Fishing e.g. Agricultural worker; bottler; craftsman's mate/labourer; finisher; fisherman; forest worker; gardener; groundsman; machine operator/assistant/attendant/minder; market garden work; motor vehicle mechanic (semi-skilled); packer; repetitive assembler; road surfacer; spinner; viewer; winder.

h) Other General Labouring

Table 2 **Comparison of the occupational classification used in the young people survey with the list of key occupations for statistical purposes contained in the classification of occupations and Directory of Occupational Titles**

Kos major occupational group	Kos group No	Survey occupational group	Survey group
Managerial (general management)	I	Managerial	A
Professional and related supporting management and administration	II		
Professional and related in education, welfare and health	III	Professional and related	B
Literary, artistic and sports	IV		
Professional and related in Science engineering, technology and other fields	V		

Kos major occupational group	Kos group No	Survey occupational group	Survey group
Managerial (excluding general management)	VI	Managerial	A
Clerical and related	VII	Clerical and related	C
Selling	VIII	Other non-manual	D
Security and protective service	IX		
Catering, cleaning, hairdressing and other personal services	X	Manual occupation in service or transport	F
Farming, fishing and related	XI	KOS groups XI to XVI split in accordance with DE unemployment vacancy classification – see paragraph 1. 2 above.	E
Materials processing, excluding metal	XII		
Making and repairing (excluding metal and electrical)	XIII		
Processing, making, repairing and related (metal and electrical)	XIV	E. Craft and similar	G
Painting, repetitive assembling, product inspecting, packaging and related	XV	G. Other manual	
Construction, mining, and related not identified elsewhere	XVI		
Transport operating, materials moving and storing and related	XVII	Manual occupations in service or transport	F
Miscellaneous	XVIII	General labourers, NEC	H

Table 3 **Industrial classifications used in the surveys**

Industry	1968 SIC order	Classification employed in Employers Survey	Classification employed in Young People and Unemployed Surveys
Agriculture and forestry	I		Basic industries
Mining and quarrying	II		
Food, drink and tobacco	III		
Coal and petroleum products	IV	Process	Manufacturing industries
Chemicals and allied industries	V		

Industry	1968 SIC order	Classification employed in Employers Survey	Classification employed in Young People and Unemployed Surveys
Metal manufacture	VI		
Mechanical engineering	VII		
Instrument engineering	VIII		
Electrical engineering	IX	Fabrication	
Shipbuilding and marine engineering	X		
Vehicles	XI		Manufacturing industries
Metal Goods N.E.S.	XII		
Textiles	XIII		
Leather, leather goods and fur	XIV	Textiles, leather and clothing	
Clothing and footwear	XV		
Bricks, pottery, cement, glass, etc	XVI	Other manufacturing industries	
Timber, furniture, etc	XVII		
Paper, printing and publishing	XVIII	Process	
Other manufacturing industries	XIX	Other manufacturing	
Construction	XX	Construction	Construction and building industries
Gas, electricity and water	XXI	Utilities and transport	Gas, electricity and water
Transport and communications	XXII		Distribution and transport and communication
Distributive trades	XXIII	Distribution	
Insurance, banking and finance	XXIV	Finance and business services	Insurance, banking and other business services
Professional, scientific services	XXV	Professional, scientific and consumer services	Professional and scientific services
Miscellaneous services	XXVI		Other services
Public administration and defence	XXVII	Local administration (N.B. excludes Central govt.)	Central and local government

References

1 Department of Employment. At Odds. The employment problems of disadvantaged young people. 1970.

2 Daniel W. W., A National Survey of the Unemployed. PEP 1974.

3 Harrison, R. The demoralising experience of prolonged unemployment. In Department of Employment Gazette. April 1976. (Summarises recent research).
Hill J. M. M. The Social and Psychological Impact of Unemployment.
Tavistock Institute of Human Relations. April 1977. Unpublished.

4 Manpower Services Commission, Young People and Work: a report on the feasibility of a new programme of opportunities for unemployed young people. 1977.

5 Ibid.

6 Department of Education and Science, Statistics of Education 1976, Vol II. To be published.

7 Fogelman, K. (Ed), Britain's Sixteen Year Olds. National Children's Bureau 1976.

8 Cherry, N. Persistant job changing – is it a problem ? Journal of Occupational Psychology. 1976.
Thomas, R. K. and Wetherall, D. C. Report on stages II and III of a Youth Employment Study. To be published by OPCS.

9 Fogelman, K. op cit.

10 Brown, H., The Transition from school to work. Community Development Project Occasional Paper No 8 1973.
Cherry, N., Douglas, J. W. B. and Glass, D. V. Young School leavers at work and college. MRC report to SSRC 1971.
Fogelman, K. op cit.
Maizels, J., Adolescent needs and the transition from school to work. Athlone Press 1970.
Thomas, R. K. and Wetherall, D. C. OPCS. Looking forward to work.

11 Department of Education and Science, Careers Education in Secondary Schools: Education Survey 18. HMSO 1973.

12 Rauta, I. and Hunt, A. OPCS, Fifth form girls: their hopes for the future. HMSO 1975.
Thomas, R. K. and Wetherall, D. C. op cit.

13 Carter, M. Into work. Penguin 1966.
Maizels, J. op cit.

14 Brown, M. op cit.
Cherry, N., Douglas, J. W. B. and Glass D. V. op cit.
Maizels, J. op cit.

15 Ashton, D. N. and Field, D. Young workers. Hutchinson 1976.
Maizels, J. op cit.
Willis, P. The Main Reality. Report to SSRC. University of Birmingham. Stencilled Occasional Papers.

16 Manpower Services Commission. op cit.

17 Department of Employment, Unqualified, untrained and unemployed. HMSO 1974.

18 Keil, E. T. Becoming a worker. Leicestershire Committee for Education and Industry/ Training Services Agency 1976.

19 Baxter, J. L., The Chronic Job Changer: a study of youth unemployment. Social and Economic Administration. Vol. 9, No. 3 1975.
Cherry, N., Douglas, J. W. B. and Glass, D. V. op cit.
Maizels, J., op cit.
(The MRC study found that about 20% of job changes before the respondent's 18th birthday and involved a "down grading", around 50% no change and 30% an increase in occupational skill and status. Maizels study however, identified a more frequent "downward shift in skill and status of occupations, mainly due to the movement of apprentices and non-manual workers leaving their first jobs and then remaining in other types of employment", though this referred to a rather small sample. Baxter's study of "Chronic job changers" a group prone to unemployment found that as high a proportion as 65% of such young people had changed to jobs which were lower skill than those initially entered).

20 Office of Population Censuses and Surveys. General Household Survey 1973. HMSO 1976.

21 Brannen, P. (Ed.), Entering the world of work: some sociological perspectives. HMSO 1975. (Summarises current theory).

22 Thomas, R. K. and Wetheral, D. C. Report on stages II and III of a Youth Employment Study. To be published by OPCS.

23 Ashton, D. N. and Field, D. op cit.
Maizels, J. op cit.

24 Keil, E. T. op cit.

25 Cherry, N., Douglas, J. W. B. and Glass, D. V. op cit.

26 Training Services Agency, Vocational Preparation for Young People. 1975.

27 Cherry, N., Douglas, J. W. B. and Glass D. V. op cit.
28 Ibid.
29 Thomas, R. K. and Wetherall, D. C. op cit.
30 Cherry, N., Douglas, J. W. B. and Glass D. V. op cit.
   Thomas, R. K. and Wetherall, D. C. op cit.
31 Department of Employment, Classification of Occupations and Directory of Occupational Titles. HMSO 1972.

Bibliography

Ashton, D. N., and Field, D.,
Young Workers. Hutchinson 1976.

Baxter, J. L.,
The Chronic Job Changer: a study of youth unemployment, in Social and Economic Administration. Vol. 9, No 3 1975.

Bazalgette, J.,
School-life and work-life in the inner city. Hutchinsons, in press.

Brannen, P. (ED),
Entering the World of Work: some sociological perspectives. HMSO 1975.

Brown, H.,
The transition from school to work. Community Development Project Occasional Paper No 8 1973.

Carter, M.,
Into Work. Penguin 1966.

Cherry, N.,
Do Careers Officers give good advice? British Journal of Guidance and Counselling, Vol. 2 No. 1 January 1974.

Cherry, N.,
Persistant Job Changing – is it a problem? in Journal of Occupational Psychology 1976.

Cherry, N., Glass, D. V. and Douglas, J. W. B.,
Young school leavers at work and college. MRC report submitted to S.S. R.C. 1971.

Daniel, W. W.,
A National Survey of the Unemployed. PEP 1974.

Douglas, J. W. B., Ross, J. M. and Simpson, H. R.,
All our future. Peter Davies 1968.

Education and Science, Department of,
Careers Education in secondary schools: Education Survey 18. HMSO 1973.

Employment, Department of,
At Odds. The employment problems of disadvantaged young people. DE 1970.

Employment, Department of,
Unqualified, untrained and unemployed. HMSO 1974.

Fogelman, K. (ED),
Britain's Sixteen-Year-Olds, National Children's Bureau 1976.

Harrison, R.,
The demoralising experience of prolonged unemployment. Department of Employment Gazette. April 1976.

Hill, J. M. M.,
The social and psychological impact of unemployment. Tavistock Institute of Human Relations for the Manpower Services Commission. April 1977. Unpublished.

Keil, E. T.,
Becoming a worker. Leicestershire Committee for Education and Industry/Training Services Agency 1976.

Maizels, J.,
Adolescent needs and the transition from school to work. Athlone Press 1970

Manpower Services Commission,
Young People and Work: Report on the feasibility of a New Programme of Opportunities for Unemployed Young People. MSC 1977.

Mukherjee, S.,
There's work to be done. HMSO 1974

Mungham, G., and Pearson, G. (EDs),
Working class youth culture. Routledge and Kegan Paul 1976.

Office of Population Censuses and Survey,
General Household Survey 1973. HMSO 1976

Organisation for Economic Co-operation and Development,
Entry of Young People into Working Life. OECD 1973.

Phillips, D.,
Young and unemployed in a northern city in Weir, D, Men and work in Modern Britain. Fontana 1973.

Rauta, I., and Hunt, A., OPCS,
Fifth form girls: their hopes for the future. HMSO 1975.

Rutter, M., and Madge, N.,
Cycles of Disadvantage. Heinemann Educational Books 1976.

Statistical Office of the European Communities,
Social Statistics: Labour force sample survey 1973, S.O.E.C. 1975.

Training Services Agency,
Vocational Preparation for young people. TSA 1975.

Thomas, R. K., and Wetherall, D. C., OPCS,
Looking forward to Work. HMSO 1974.

Thomas, R. K., and Wetherall, D. C., OPCS,
Report on Stages II and III of a Youth Employment Study. To be published.

Turner, B., (ED),
Truancy. Ward Lock Educational 1974.

Willis, P.,
Lads, lobes and labour, New Society, 20 May 1976.

Willis, P.,
The Main Reality. Report to SSRC. University of Birmingham. Stencilled Occasional Papers.

Employment, Department of,
Classification of Occupations and, Directory of Occupational Titles. HMSO 1972.

Prepared by the Manpower Services Commission and the Central Office of Information 1978

Printed in England for Her Majesty's Stationery Office
by Hambleden Press, St Peters Rd, Huntingdon, Cambs PE18 7DF.   Dd 554804.   Pro 9872.   K16